Buckle Down™

New York
Mathematics

Grade 4

3rd Edition

This book belongs to: _____

Buckle Down™

Helping your schoolhouse meet the standards of the statehouse™

ISBN-10: 0-7836-7072-9

ISBN-13: 978-0-7836-7072-0

3BDNY04MM01   3 4 5 6 7 8 9 10

Cover Image: ©Thinkstock

Triumph Learning® 136 Madison Avenue, 7th Floor, New York, NY 10016

© 2011 Triumph Learning, LLC
Buckle Down is an imprint of Triumph Learning®

Printed in the United States of America.

TABLE OF CONTENTS

Table of Contents

To the Teacher:

Performance Indicator numbers are listed for each lesson in the table of contents. The numbers in the shaded gray bar that runs across the tops of the pages in the workbook indicate the Standards Name for a given page (see example to the left).

Introduction

When you start thinking about all of the times and places you use your math skills, you might be surprised. How many minutes are left until school is over for the day? How much taller are you now than you were a year ago? How many points per game is the leading rusher for your favorite football team averaging? These are examples of how people use math every day.

This book will help you practice your everyday math skills. It will also help you with math that is more uncommon, like the kinds you might only see in math class and on math tests. If you practice all the math skills in this book, you will be ready to do your best on almost any math test.

Test-Taking Tips

Here are a few tips that will help you on test day.

TIP 1: Take it easy.

Stay calm and trust your math skills. You've practiced the problems in *Buckle Down*, so you are ready to do your best on almost any math test. Take a few slow, deep breaths before you begin the test.

TIP 2: Read the questions more than once.

Every question is different. Some questions are more difficult than others. If you need to, read a question more than once. This will help you make a plan for solving the problem.

TIP 3: Learn to "plug in" answers to multiple-choice items.

When do you "plug in"? You should "plug in" whenever your answer is different from all of the answer choices or you can't come up with an answer. Plug each answer choice into the problem and find the one that makes sense. (You can also think of this as "working backward.")

TIP 4: Answer open-ended items completely.

When answering short-response or extended-response items, show all your work to receive as many points as possible. Write neatly enough so that your work will be easy to follow. Make sure your answer is clearly marked.

TIP 5: Check your work.

Take the time to check your work on every problem. By checking your work, you can find and fix careless mistakes.

TIP 6: Use all the test time.

Work on the test until you are told to stop. If you finish early, go back through the test and double-check your answers. You just might improve your score on the test by finding and fixing any errors you might have made.

Unit 1

Number Sense and Operations

You may not realize it, but you use your number sense many times a day. You solve problems using numbers when you figure out how much time you have to get ready for school, about how much money you will need for a movie ticket and a box of popcorn, or whether it will be warm enough to go swimming. Having number sense helps you to understand things such as time, money, and temperature. Numbers are important in almost every part of your life.

In this unit, you will solve problems involving addition, subtraction, multiplication, and division. You will learn about the relationships between numbers, including whole numbers, decimals, and fractions. You will review estimation and learn some strategies for problem solving.

In This Unit

Whole Numbers

Computation with
    Whole Numbers

Fractions

Decimals

Estimation and
    Problem Solving

Lesson 1: Whole Numbers

A **whole number** is a number that shows ones, tens, hundreds, thousands, and so on.

Representing Whole Numbers

You can write a whole number using digits, words, or models.

Digits and Words

0, 1, 2, 3, 4, 5, 6, 7, 8, and 9 are the digits used to write whole numbers.

The number 1,247 has four digits: 1   2   4   7

The number 1,247 is written in **standard form**.

In **word form**, the number 1,247 is written *one thousand, two hundred forty-seven*.

Models

Numbers can be shown using models.

These blocks represent the number 1,247.

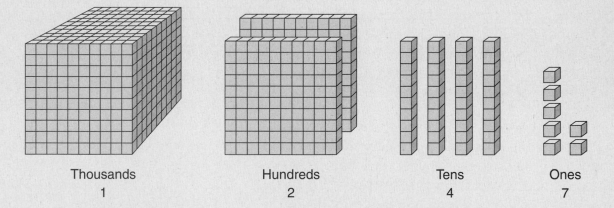

Thousands	Hundreds	Tens	Ones
1	2	4	7

TIP: Commas separate groups of digits so that you can easily read large numbers. Start at the far right of the number. Work your way left. Place a comma to the left of every 3rd digit.

3,1 8 4 ← start
3 2 1

Place Value

Each digit has a value based on its place in a number. Place-value tables show the values of the digits of a number.

Example

This place-value table shows how many thousands, hundreds, tens, and ones are in 3,400.

Thousands	Hundreds	Tens	Ones
3	4	0	0

The digit 3 in the thousands column shows that there are 3 thousands in 3,400. The digit 4 in the hundreds column shows that there are 4 hundreds in 3,400. The zeros written in the tens and ones columns show that there are zero (0) tens and 0 ones in 3,400.

Example

This place-value table shows the values of the digits of 8,041.

Thousands	Hundreds	Tens	Ones
8	0	4	1

Numbers written in **expanded form** show the values of the digits. Notice that there are no hundreds. This is why a 0 (zero) is written in that place. Zeros are not shown in expanded form or written in word form.

$8,041 = 8,000 + 40 + 1$

$8,041 = $ eight thousand, forty-one
⬆
└─ hundreds

Example

This list shows a pattern of skip counting by 1,000s.

1,750   **2**,750   **3**,750   **4**,750

The only digit that changes is the digit in the thousands place.

Practice

1. Write the standard, expanded, and word forms of the number represented by the model below.

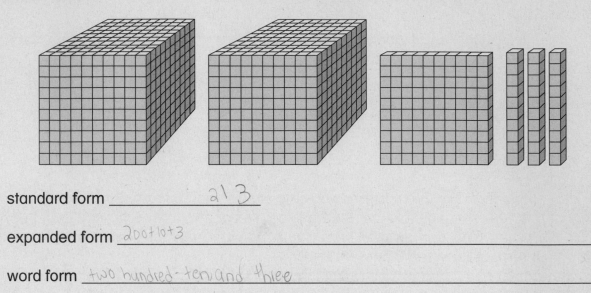

standard form _____ 213 _____

expanded form _____ 200+10+3 _____

word form _____ two hundred-ten and three _____

2. Write the digits of the following numbers in the correct places in the table.

4,736   8,039   5,973

Thousands	Hundreds	Tens	Ones

Directions: For questions 3 through 5, write the numbers in word form and expanded form.

3. 4,736

word form _____

expanded form _____

4. 8,039

   word form _____

   expanded form _____

5. 5,973

   word form _____

   expanded form _____

Directions: For questions 6 through 8, fill in the missing numbers.

6. 1,456   2,456   3,456   _____   5,456

7. 3,705   _____   5,705   _____   7,705

8. _____   6,320   7,320   _____   9,320

9. In the number 7,482, what digit is in the thousands place?

   A. 2

   B. 4

   C. 7

   D. 8

10. Which number is 1,000 more than 2,306?

   A. 1,306

   B. 2,307

   C. 3,306

   D. 3,417

11. How is eight thousand, four hundred written in standard form?

   A. 4,800

   B. 8,004

   C. 8,040

   D. 8,400

12. Which pattern shows skip counting by 1,000s?

   A. 4,162; 5,273; 6,384

   B. 4,162; 5,162; 6,162

   C. 4,162; 4,262; 4,362

   D. 4,162; 4,163; 4,164

Equivalent Representations of Whole Numbers

When you write a number in expanded form, you are **decomposing** the number. When you add numbers together, you are **composing** a number. Writing a number in expanded form is only one way to decompose a number. Most numbers can be decomposed in several ways. Each of these ways is called an **equivalent representation** of the number.

Examples

The expanded form of the number 4,384 is $4,000 + 300 + 80 + 4$.

There are many other ways to decompose the number 4,384. The following are just two of the many equivalent representations of the number 4,384.

$2,000 + 2,000 + 150 + 150 + 80 + 4$

$3,000 + 1,000 + 250 + 100 + 30 + 2 + 2$

These representations are called "equivalent" because they have the same sum. In this case, the sum is 4,384.

Examples

Add $850 + 600 + 25 + 4$ to compose a number.

$850 + 600 + 25 + 4 = 1,479$

Add $1,000 + 400 + 70 + 9$ to compose a number.

$1,000 + 400 + 70 + 9 = 1,479$

These are just two of the ways to compose 1,479.

Directions: For questions 1 and 2, write two equivalent representations of the given number.

1. 376 _____

2. 1,750 _____

Directions: For questions 3 and 4, compose the given number.

3. $6,000 + 2,500 + 700 + 64$ _____

4. $900 + 300 + 75 + 66$ _____

Performance Indicators: 4.N.3, 4.A.2

Comparing and Ordering Whole Numbers

When you compare two numbers, you decide which number is **greater than** the other or which number is **less than** the other. Sometimes when you compare two numbers, you find that the numbers are **equal**.

Signs for Comparison

The signs that are used to compare numbers are $<$, $>$, and $=$.

$<$ means **is less than**

$>$ means **is greater than**

$=$ means **is equal to**

Place-Value Tables

You can compare and order whole numbers using a place-value table. Compare the digits in each place-value position from left to right and look for digits that are different.

Example

In the following place-value table, the numbers have the same digits in the thousands and hundreds place. The digits are all different in the tens place.

Thousands	Hundreds	Tens	Ones
3	4	**4**	3
3	4	**2**	4
3	4	**7**	1

The digit 4 is greater than the digit 2, so $3,443 > 3,424$.

The digit 2 is less than the digit 7, so $3,424 < 3,471$.

The digit 4 is less than the digit 7, so $3,443 < 3,471$.

The numbers in order from **least** to **greatest** are 3,424; 3,443; 3,471.

The numbers in order from **greatest** to **least** are 3,471; 3,443; 3,424.

Number Lines

Another way to compare and order whole numbers is to use a number line. A number to the right of another number on a number line is **greater** in value. A number to the left of another number on a number line is **lesser** in value.

Example

Compare 679 and 745.

Look at the following number line. Where is 679 compared to 745?

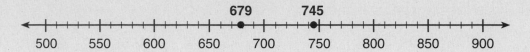

Because 679 is to the left of 745, you can say that 679 is **less** than 745.

679 < 745

You can also say that 745 is **greater** than 679 (because 745 is to the right of 679 on the number line).

745 > 679

Example

Order the numbers 265, 256, and 273 from **least** to **greatest**.

Place the numbers on a number line.

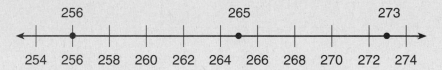

256 is to the left of 265, and 265 is to the left of 273. The numbers in order from **least** to **greatest** are 256, 265, 273.

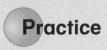 **Practice**

Directions: For questions 1 through 4, use the table below to compare the numbers. Write the correct symbol (>, <, or =) on the blank.

Thousands	Hundreds	Tens	Ones
8	5	2	6
8	7	0	1
8	4	9	3

1. 8,526 _____ 8,493

2. 8,701 _____ 8,526

3. 8,493 _____ 8,701

4. Write the numbers in the table in order from **greatest** to **least**.

_____

5. Write the following numbers in the correct place on the number line.

    442   454   439   437

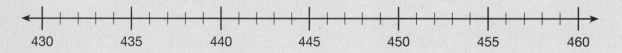

430   435   440   445   450   455   460

6. Write the numbers on the number line in order from **least** to **greatest**.

_____

Directions: For questions 7 through 9, use the number line above to compare the numbers. Write the correct symbol (>, <, or =) on the blank.

7. 442 _____ 440

8. 440 _____ 439

9. 454 _____ 450

10. Write the following numbers in the correct place on the number line.

   1,002   989   1,009   996

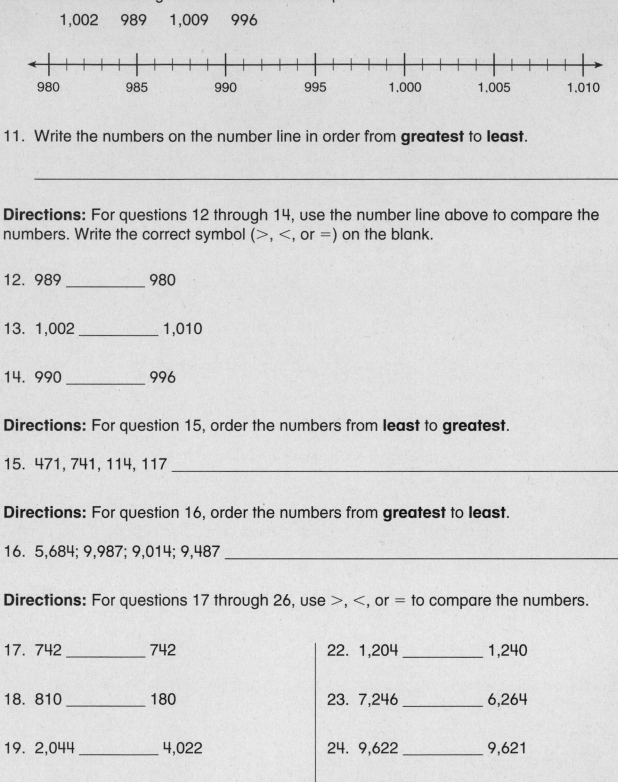

11. Write the numbers on the number line in order from **greatest** to **least**.

_____

Directions: For questions 12 through 14, use the number line above to compare the numbers. Write the correct symbol (>, <, or =) on the blank.

12. 989 _____ 980

13. 1,002 _____ 1,010

14. 990 _____ 996

Directions: For question 15, order the numbers from **least** to **greatest**.

15. 471, 741, 114, 117 _____

Directions: For question 16, order the numbers from **greatest** to **least**.

16. 5,684; 9,987; 9,014; 9,487 _____

Directions: For questions 17 through 26, use >, <, or = to compare the numbers.

17. 742 _____ 742

18. 810 _____ 180

19. 2,044 _____ 4,022

20. 1,539 _____ 1,695

21. 8,513 _____ 8,315

22. 1,204 _____ 1,240

23. 7,246 _____ 6,264

24. 9,622 _____ 9,621

25. 7,118 _____ 7,119

26. 7,843 _____ 7,843

New York Math Practice

1 Which is the standard form of the number represented by the model shown below?

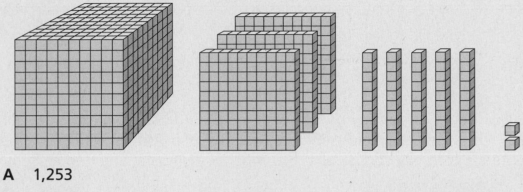

A 1,253

B 1,352

C 2,135

D 2,531

2 Kate writes an equivalent representation of 5,050 on the board. Which of these representations could Kate have written?

A 4,000 + 100 + 50

B 2,500 + 2,500 + 40 + 20

C 3,000 + 2,000 + 35 + 15

D 4,200 + 900 + 25 + 25

3 Jamal, Lin, Tiffany, and Bill played a video game. The points they scored are shown in the table below.

Jamal	Lin	Tiffany	Bill
2,711	2,171	2,117	2,177

Which list shows the points scored in order from **greatest** to **least**?

A 2,117   2,171   2,177   2,711

B 2,711   2,177   2,171   2,117

C 2,177   2,117   2,171   2,711

D 2,711   2,117   2,171   2,177

4 Bernie told his class that he has three thousand, forty-two stamps in his collection. What is the standard form of the number of stamps Bernie has in his collection?

A 3,42

B 3,420

C 3,402

D 3,042

5 The Museum of the City of New York had 5,380 visitors on one day. On the same day, the Queens Museum of Art had 5,308 visitors. Which number sentence correctly compares the number of visitors at the two museums?

A 5,308 < 5,380

B 5,380 = 5,308

C 5,308 > 5,380

D 5,380 < 5,308

6 Ali is playing a number game. He has number cards for 8, 4, 9, and 2. What is the **greatest** number Ali can make with these cards?

A 9,824

B 2,489

C 8,249

D 9,842

7 Carla writes 9,000 + 40 + 6 in standard form on her paper. Which of these numbers could Carla have written?

A 946

B 964

C 9,046

D 9,406

8 Which of these numbers has a 4 in the thousands place and a 6 in the ones place?

A 4,206

B 4,602

C 6,204

D 6,420

9 Adam is writing a number pattern. Which number belongs on the line below to complete the pattern?

2,798   3,798   ___?___   5,798

A 3,799

B 3,898

C 4,798

D 6,798

10 The number of pennies collected by each fourth-grade class at Hudson Valley School is shown below.

1,035   1,040   940   995   1,080

Write the numbers of pennies on the number line below. Then write the number of pennies in order from **least** to **greatest**.

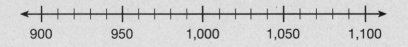

Answer _____

Lesson 2: Computation with Whole Numbers

In this lesson, you will review how to add, subtract, multiply, and divide whole numbers.

Addition

The answer to an addition problem is the **sum**. The numbers that are added are **addends**. To find the sum, line up the digits with the same place values. Remember to regroup when necessary.

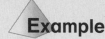

Example

Add: 5,252 + 2,495

Line up the place values.

$$\begin{array}{r} 5{,}252 \\ +\ 2{,}495 \\ \hline \end{array}$$

Add the ones.

$$\begin{array}{r} 5{,}25\mathbf{2} \\ +\ 2{,}49\mathbf{5} \\ \hline \mathbf{7} \end{array}$$

Add the tens. Regroup the hundreds.

$$\begin{array}{r} {}^{1} \\ 5{,}2\mathbf{5}2 \\ +\ 2{,}4\mathbf{9}5 \\ \hline \mathbf{4}7 \end{array}$$

Add the hundreds.

$$\begin{array}{r} {}^{1} \\ 5{,}\mathbf{2}52 \\ +\ 2{,}\mathbf{4}95 \\ \hline \mathbf{7}47 \end{array}$$

Add the thousands.

$$\begin{array}{r} {}^{1} \\ \mathbf{5}{,}252 \\ +\ \mathbf{2}{,}495 \\ \hline \mathbf{7}{,}747 \end{array}$$

Therefore, 5,252 + 2,495 = 7,747.

Practice

Directions: For questions 1 through 6, line up the digits with the same place values and then add.

1. 95 + 33 = _____

2. 764 + 681 = _____

3. 7,946 + 1,275 = _____

4. 5,297 + 2,031 = _____

5. 27 + 1,974 = _____

6. 1,554 + 848 = _____

Directions: For questions 7 and 8, find the sum.

7. Last year, Mr. Sheldon's class recycled 2,023 cans. This year, the class recycled 7,008 cans. How many cans did the class recycle in both years combined?

_____

8. The Buffalo Zoo had 4,802 visitors last weekend. The Bronx Zoo had 3,219 visitors last weekend. How many visitors went to the two zoos combined?

_____

Subtraction

The answer to a subtraction problem is the **difference**. When finding the difference, remember to line up the place values and regroup when necessary.

Example

Subtract: 5,189 − 3,242

Line up the place values.

$$\begin{array}{r} 5,189 \\ -\ 3,242 \\ \hline \end{array}$$

Subtract the ones.

$$\begin{array}{r} 5,18\mathbf{9} \\ -\ 3,24\mathbf{2} \\ \hline \mathbf{7} \end{array}$$

Subtract the tens.

$$\begin{array}{r} 5,1\mathbf{8}9 \\ -\ 3,2\mathbf{4}2 \\ \hline \mathbf{4}7 \end{array}$$

Regroup 1 thousand. Then subtract the hundreds.

$$\begin{array}{r} {}^{4}\!\!\!\!\!{}^{11} \\ \cancel{5},\!\cancel{1}89 \\ -\ 3,\mathbf{2}42 \\ \hline \mathbf{9}47 \end{array}$$

Finally, subtract the thousands.

$$\begin{array}{r} {}^{4}\!\!\!\!\!{}^{11} \\ \cancel{5},\!\cancel{1}89 \\ -\ \mathbf{3},242 \\ \hline \mathbf{1},947 \end{array}$$

Therefore, 5,189 − 3,242 = 1,947.

Practice

Directions: For questions 1 through 6, line up the digits with the same place values and then subtract.

1. 95 − 13 = _____

2. 951 − 242 = _____

3. 5,080 − 1,457 = _____

4. 5,630 − 3,492 = _____

5. 8,204 − 983 = _____

6. 627 − 79 = _____

Directions: For questions 7 and 8, find the difference.

7. Arturo had 1,825 baseball cards. He sold 872 of them at a baseball card show. How many baseball cards does Arturo have left?

_____

8. Last year, 4,420 people signed up for the Fun Day Race. This year, 2,183 people signed up for the race. How many more people signed up for the race last year than this year?

_____

Multiplication

The answer to a multiplication problem is a **product**. The numbers you multiply are **factors**. Here is one way to write a multiplication fact:

$$3 \times 4 = 12$$

factors   product

Multiplication Strategies

Grouping can be used to multiply. After you group items together, you can either **skip count** or use **repeated addition** to find the total number of items.

Example

How many DVDs are there? Separate the DVDs into groups of 3.

You can use skip counting to find the total number of DVDs.

3, 6, 9, 12

You can use a repeated addition sentence to show the number of DVDs.

$$3 + 3 + 3 + 3 = 12$$

You can use a multiplication number sentence to show the number of DVDs.

$$4 \times 3 = 12$$

There are 12 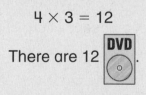.

Another way to show multiplication is to use arrays. An **array** is a group of objects that are arranged in rows and columns in the shape of a rectangle.

Example

How many pencils are there?

One way to find the answer is to count all the pencils. But this can take a long time, especially when there are a lot of objects. Instead, you can count the number of rows and the number of columns and then multiply.

There are 3 rows of pencils. This is the first factor.

There are 5 pencils in every row. This is the second factor.

$3 \times 5 = 15$

There are 15 pencils. You can check this by counting all the pencils.

You can also show multiplication using an area model. An **area model** is a rectangle made of squares that are each 1 unit by 1 unit.

Example

What multiplication problem is shown by the area model below?

8

2

The length of the rectangle is 8 units. This is the first factor.

The width of the rectangle is 2 units. This is the second factor.

The area model shows $8 \times 2 = 16$. You can check this by counting all the squares.

Practice

Directions: Use the following drawing to answer questions 1 and 2.

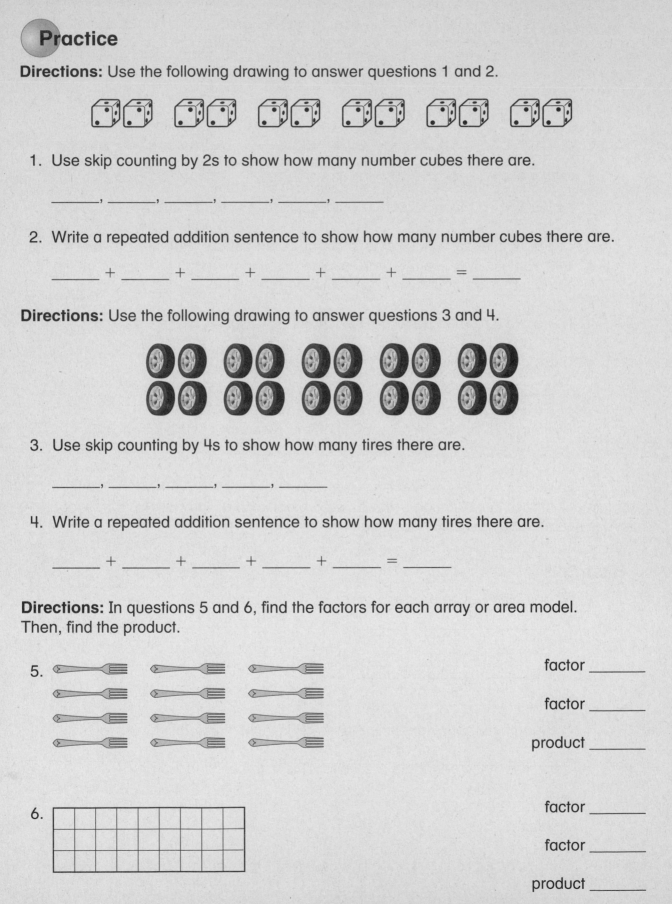

1. Use skip counting by 2s to show how many number cubes there are.

   _____, _____, _____, _____, _____, _____

2. Write a repeated addition sentence to show how many number cubes there are.

   _____ + _____ + _____ + _____ + _____ + _____ = _____

Directions: Use the following drawing to answer questions 3 and 4.

3. Use skip counting by 4s to show how many tires there are.

   _____, _____, _____, _____, _____

4. Write a repeated addition sentence to show how many tires there are.

   _____ + _____ + _____ + _____ + _____ = _____

Directions: In questions 5 and 6, find the factors for each array or area model. Then, find the product.

5.

factor _____

factor _____

product _____

6.

factor _____

factor _____

product _____

Performance Indicator: 4.N.16

Basic Multiplication Facts

Knowing your basic multiplication facts is important for working multiplication problems that have greater numbers.

Practice

1. Fill in the multiplication table. Multiply a number in the top row times a number in the left column. Write the product in the box where the row and column meet.

×	1	2	3	4	5	6	7	8	9	10	11	12
1												
2												
3												
4												
5												
6												
7												
8												
9												
10												
11												
12												

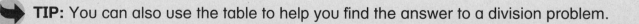 **TIP:** You can also use the table to help you find the answer to a division problem.

Multiplying by One-Digit Numbers

Sometimes you want to multiply numbers greater than the ones in your multiplication table. You can follow the steps below to multiply two-digit numbers.

 Example

Line up the digits with the same place values.

$$\begin{array}{r} 23 \\ \times2 \\ \hline \end{array}$$

Multiply the ones by 2: 3 ones $\times$ 2 = 6 ones. Write a 6 in the ones place.

$$\begin{array}{r} 23 \\ \times2 \\ \hline 6 \end{array}$$

Multiply the tens by 2: 2 tens $\times$ 2 = 4 tens. Write a 4 in the tens place.

$$\begin{array}{r} 23 \\ \times2 \\ \hline 46 \end{array}$$

 Example

Line up the digits with the same place values.

$$\begin{array}{r} 75 \\ \times8 \\ \hline \end{array}$$

Multiply the ones by 8: 5 ones $\times$ 8 = 40 ones. Write a 0 and regroup the 4 tens.

$$\begin{array}{r} 4 \\ 75 \\ \times8 \\ \hline 0 \end{array}$$

Multiply the tens by 8: 7 tens $\times$ 8 = 56 tens. Then add the 4 tens to the 56 tens: 4 + 56 = 60. Write a 0 in the tens place. Write a 6 in the hundreds place.

$$\begin{array}{r} 4 \\ 75 \\ \times8 \\ \hline 600 \end{array}$$

Practice

Directions: For questions 1 through 6, line up the digits with the same place values and then multiply.

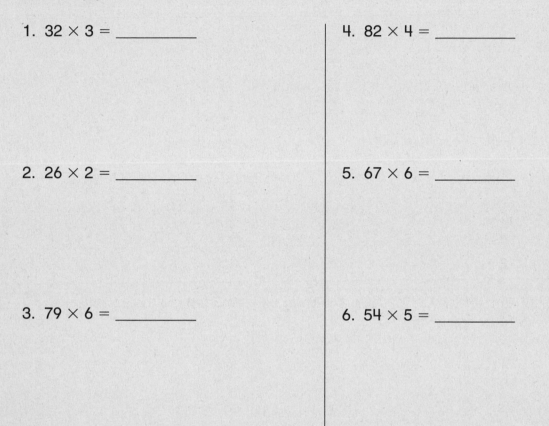

1. $32 \times 3 =$ _____

2. $26 \times 2 =$ _____

3. $79 \times 6 =$ _____

4. $82 \times 4 =$ _____

5. $67 \times 6 =$ _____

6. $54 \times 5 =$ _____

Directions: For questions 7 and 8, find the product.

7. The dinosaur triceratops had 3 horns. How many horns could you find in a herd of 85 triceratops?

_____

8. Wanda has 4 pages of math problems to do for homework. There are 28 problems on each page. How many math problems does Wanda have to do?

_____

Multiplying by Two-Digit Numbers

You can also multiply a two-digit number by another two-digit number. You will need to multiply the first factor by each digit in the second factor and add the products together.

 Example

Multiply: 24 × 18

Line up the digits with the same place values.

$$\begin{array}{r} 24 \\ \times\ 18 \\ \hline \end{array}$$

Multiply the ones by 8: 4 × 8 = 32. Write a 2 and regroup the 3 tens.

$$\begin{array}{r} ^{3} \\ 24 \\ \times\ 18 \\ \hline 2 \end{array}$$

Multiply the tens by 8: 2 × 8 = 16. Then add the 3 tens to the 16 tens: 3 + 16 = 19. Write 19.

$$\begin{array}{r} ^{3} \\ 24 \\ \times\ 18 \\ \hline 192 \end{array}$$

Write a 0 under the 2 in 192 as a place holder. Multiply the ones by 1: 4 × 1 = 4. Write 4 under the 9 in 192.

$$\begin{array}{r} ^{3} \\ 24 \\ \times\ 18 \\ \hline 192 \\ 40 \end{array}$$

Multiply the tens by 1: 2 × 1 = 2. Write 2 under the 1 in 192. Then add 192 and 240.

$$\begin{array}{r} ^{3} \\ 24 \\ \times\ 18 \\ \hline 192 \\ +\ 240 \\ \hline 432 \end{array}$$

Practice

Directions: For questions 1 through 6, line up the digits with the same place values and then multiply.

1. 42 × 13 = _____

2. 38 × 28 = _____

3. 92 × 53 = _____

4. 75 × 27 = _____

5. 56 × 38 = _____

6. 79 × 42 = _____

Directions: For questions 7 and 8, use multiplication to solve each problem.

7. Ms. Hoover's class of 15 students visited a sticker factory. Each student was given 25 stickers. How many stickers did the entire class receive?

_____

8. A set of bleachers has 14 rows. Each row has 31 seats. How many seats are in a set of bleachers?

_____

Multiplying by Multiples of 10 and 100

A **multiple** of a number is the product of that number and another whole number.

Multiples of 10: 10 (1 × 10), 20 (2 × 10), 30 (3 × 10), and so on

Multiples of 100: 100 (1 × 100), 200 (2 × 100), 300 (3 × 100), and so on

You can use multiplication facts to solve problems that have a multiple of 10 or 100 as a factor.

Example

Use a multiplication fact and a pattern of zeros to solve 7 × 400.

7 × 4 = 28

7 × **4**0 = 28**0**

7 × **4**00 = 2,8**00**

You can also use this rule: **Remove any zeros from the factors, and multiply just the nonzero digits. Then put the zeros back onto the product.**

Examples

3 × 6**0** → 3 × 6 = 18 → 18**0** (Replace the zero.)

4**0** × 2**0** → 4 × 2 = 8 → 8**00** (Replace the two zeros.)

2**00** × 11 → 2 × 11 = 22 → 2,2**00** (Replace the two zeros.)

Practice

Directions: For questions 1 through 10, find the product.

1. 4 × 40 = _____

2. 3 × 90 = _____

3. 500 × 7 = _____

4. 90 × 20 = _____

5. 40 × 50 = _____

6. 7 × 100 = _____

7. 50 × 5 = _____

8. 1,100 × 2 = _____

9. 70 × 80 = _____

10. 6 × 600 = _____

Associative Property of Multiplication

The **associative property of multiplication** states that the **grouping** of the factors does not change the product of a multiplication problem.

$$(3 \times 2) \times 5 = 3 \times (2 \times 5)$$
$$6 \times 5 = 3 \times 10$$
$$30 = 30$$

Example

Use the associative property of multiplication to simplify the problem.

$$(12 \times 20) \times 10$$

Regroup the multiplication problem so that the simpler multiplication is done first: 20×10. Then multiply by 12.

$$12 \times (20 \times 10) = 12 \times 200$$
$$= 2,400$$

Practice

Directions: For questions 1 through 6, use the associative property of multiplication to fill in the blanks.

1. $2 \times (4 \times 3) = (\underline{} \times 4) \times 3$

2. $(7 \times 5) \times 6 = 7 \times (\underline{} \times 6)$

3. $(8 \times \underline{}) \times 5 = 8 \times (20 \times 5)$

4. $3 \times (7 \times \underline{}) = (\underline{} \times 7) \times 4$

5. $(5 \times \underline{}) \times 4 = 5 \times (25 \times \underline{})$

6. $(11 \times 30) \times \underline{} = \underline{} \times (30 \times 10)$

Directions: For questions 7 through 12, use the associative property of multiplication to simplify.

7. $(9 \times 50) \times 2 = \underline{}$

8. $20 \times (5 \times 12) = \underline{}$

9. $4 \times (25 \times 7) = \underline{}$

10. $(9 \times 30) \times 10 = \underline{}$

11. $40 \times (20 \times 6) = \underline{}$

12. $(12 \times 60) \times 10 = \underline{}$

Even and Odd Numbers

Even numbers are numbers with 0, 2, 4, 6, or 8 in the ones place.

Odd numbers are numbers with 1, 3, 5, 7, or 9 in the ones place.

When you multiply two numbers, you can tell whether the product will be even or odd by looking at whether the factors are even or odd. If at least one of the two factors is even, then the product will be even.

Examples

When both factors are even, the product will be even.

2 (even) × 6 (even) = 12 (even)

When both factors are odd, the product will be odd.

3 (odd) × 5 (odd) = 15 (odd)

When one factor is even and one factor is odd, the product will be even.

4 (even) × 7 (odd) = 28 (even)

Practice

Directions: For questions 1 through 8, write whether the product will be *even* or *odd*.

1. 64 × 71 _____

2. 19 × 33 _____

3. 12 × 81 _____

4. 45 × 97 _____

5. 382 × 6 _____

6. odd × even _____

7. even × even _____

8. odd × odd _____

Division

The answer to a division problem is the **quotient**. The number you are dividing by is the **divisor**. The number you are dividing into is the **dividend**. The number that is left over, if there is one, is the **remainder**. Here are two ways to write division facts:

quotient → 4
divisor → 6)24
           ↑
        dividend

$24 \div 6 = 4$ ← quotient
  ↑   ↑
dividend divisor

Division Strategies

Grouping can be used to divide. Divide the total into groups of the same size. If there is anything left over, it is the remainder. You can also use **repeated subtraction** to show the groupings.

Example

Divide 13 nickels into groups of 4.

There are 3 groups of 4, and there is 1 left over.

$13 \div 4 = 3\ R1$

Use repeated subtraction to show the number of groups.

$13 - 4 = 9$ **(1 time)**

$9 - 4 = 5$ **(2 times)**

$5 - 4 = 1$ **(3 times)**

There are 3 groups of 4, and there is 1 left over.

$13 \div 4 = 3\ R1$

You can also use **equal sharing** to divide. Place one object in each group. Repeat this until all the objects are in a group. The number of objects in each group is the quotient.

Example

Claire has 9 pizza slices left over from a party. She wants to share them with 2 friends and have some for herself, so she needs to divide the pizza slices into 3 equal groups. How many pizza slices will be in each group?

Number the slices 1 through 3 until each slice has a number.

Count how many pizza slices have each number. This is how many slices will be in each group, or the number of slices that each person will get.

There are three 1s, three 2s, and three 3s.

Each person will get 3 pizza slices. There will be 3 pizza slices in each group.

$9 \div 3 = 3$

Practice

1. Divide the toothbrushes into groups of 4. How many groups of 4 are there? Are there any left over?

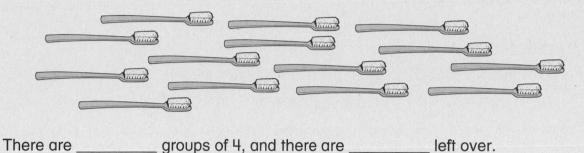

There are _____ groups of 4, and there are _____ left over.

2. Divide the books into 5 equal groups. How many books are in each group?

There are _____ books in each group.

3. In the space below, use repeated subtraction to find the answer to 25 ÷ 5.

25 ÷ 5 = _____

4. In the space below, use repeated subtraction to find the answer to 19 ÷ 4.

19 ÷ 4 = _____

Relating Multiplication and Division

Multiplication and division are opposite, or **inverse**, operations. Multiply any two numbers. Then take the product and divide it by one of the numbers. The quotient will be the other number. These 3 numbers, along with the operations of multiplication and division, form a fact family.

Example

Write the multiplication and division fact family for 4, 5, and 20.

$4 \times 5 = 20$ $20 \div 4 = 5$

$5 \times 4 = 20$ $20 \div 5 = 4$

Practice

Directions: For questions 1 through 3, fill in the blanks to complete the fact family.

1. $8 \times 5 = 40$ _____

    _____   _____

2. $24 \div 4 = 6$ _____

    _____   _____

3. $3 \times 7 = 21$ _____

    _____   _____

4. Which is part of the fact family for 4, 8, and 32?

    A. $2 \times 4 = 8$

    B. $4 \times 32 = 128$

    C. $8 \div 4 = 2$

    D. $32 \div 4 = 8$

5. Which multiplication fact could you use to solve $36 \div 9$?

    A. $3 \times 9 = 27$

    B. $6 \times 6 = 36$

    C. $9 \times 4 = 36$

    D. $36 \times 9 = 234$

Performance Indicator: 4.N.21

Dividing Two-Digit Numbers

As when multiplying greater numbers, you can divide greater numbers by following a few steps.

Example

Divide: 6)57

Divide and multiply.

        9 ← **How many 6s are in 57?**
    6)57
    − 54 ← **Multiply: 6 × 9 = 54**

Subtract and write any remainder.

        9 R3
    6)57
    − 54
        3 ← **The remainder (R) must be less than the divisor.**

Therefore, 57 ÷ 6 = 9 R3.

Example

Divide: 34 ÷ 2

Choose a way to write the problem.

    2)34

Divide and multiply.

        1 ← **How many 2s are in 3?**
    2)34
    − 2 ← **Multiply: 2 × 1 = 2**

Subtract and bring down the next number.

        1
    2)34
    − 2↓
       14

Divide, multiply, and subtract again.

       17
    2)34
    − 2↓
       14
    − 14
        0

Therefore, 34 ÷ 2 = 17.

Example

Mrs. Damon bakes 98 rolls. She divides them equally into 4 boxes for delivery to local restaurants. How many rolls does she put in each box? How many rolls are left over?

Choose a way to write the problem.

$$4\overline{)98}$$

Divide and multiply.

       2 ← **How many 4s are in 9?**
    4)98
     − 8 ← **Multiply: 4 × 2 = 8**
    ─────

Subtract and bring down the next number.

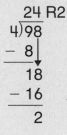

       2
    4)98
     − 8↓
    ─────
      18

Divide, multiply, and subtract again.

      24 R2
    4)98
     − 8↓
    ─────
      18
    − 16
    ─────
       2

You can use multiplication to check your answer. Multiply the quotient and the divisor. Then add the remainder.

        24
     ×   4
    ──────
        96
     + 2 ← **Don't forget to add the remainder.**
    ──────
        98 ← **This is the dividend, so your answer is correct.**

Mrs. Damon puts 24 rolls in each box. There are 2 rolls left over.

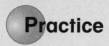Practice

Directions: For questions 1 through 10, line up the divisor and the dividend and then divide.

1. 65 ÷ 7 = _____

2. 56 ÷ 2 = _____

3. 77 ÷ 5 = _____

4. 25 ÷ 3 = _____

5. 75 ÷ 4 = _____

6. 84 ÷ 6 = _____

7. 93 ÷ 8 = _____

8. 95 ÷ 4 = _____

9. 91 ÷ 7 = _____

10. 80 ÷ 5 = _____

Directions: For questions 11 through 14, find the quotient.

11. Mr. Martin paid $87 for 3 tickets to a football game. How much did Mr. Martin pay for each ticket?

_____

12. In Huntington Station, 4 truck drivers delivered 68 boxes of vegetables. If each driver delivered the same number of boxes, how many boxes did each driver deliver?

_____

13. There are 6 small buses to take 78 campers on a field trip. If each bus carries the same number of campers, how many campers are on each bus?

_____

14. There are 84 reserved seats for a play. The seats are in the first 7 rows of one section of the theater. How many seats are in each row?

_____

15. Olga is solving the division problem below.

$$\begin{array}{r} 1 \\ 6\overline{)79} \\ -\,6 \\ \hline 1 \end{array}$$

What should Olga do next?

_____

_____

Meaning of Remainders

When solving a problem that has a remainder, it is important to know the meaning of the remainder. Sometimes you round the quotient to the next whole number, sometimes you drop the remainder and use the quotient, and sometimes the remainder is the answer.

Example

Miss Kohl has 14 paint brushes for her art class to use for a group project. Each group needs 4 paint brushes for the project. What is the greatest number of groups there can be in the class?

Divide the 14 paint brushes into groups of 4. How many groups of 4 are there?

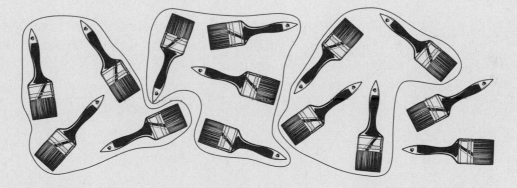

There are 3 groups of 4 paint brushes, and there are 2 left over.

$14 \div 4 = 3\ R2$

In this problem, drop the remainder because 2 paint brushes are not enough for a group to use.

There can be 3 groups in the class.

Example

Jenny is at the state fair. She has $28. Each poster at the fair costs $5. She wants to buy the maximum number of posters for the amount of money she has. How much money will Jenny have left over after buying the posters?

Divide $28 by $5.

$28 \div 5 = 5\text{ R}3$

The answer shows that Jenny can buy 5 posters, and she will have $3 left over. In this problem, the remainder is the answer.

Jenny will have $3 left over after buying the posters.

Example

Marty wants to put a wooden railing around his deck. The railing needs to be 76 feet long. Each section of railing is 8 feet long. How many sections will Marty have to buy?

Divide 76 feet by 8 feet.

$76 \div 8 = 9\text{ R}4$

In this problem, 9 sections of railing will not be enough, because Marty would still have 4 feet of his deck without a railing. Therefore, he must round up to the next whole number and buy another section of railing for the last 4 feet.

9 R4 rounded to the next whole number is 10.

Marty will have to buy 10 sections of railing.

TIP: *Left over*, *extra*, and *remaining* are clue phrases that the problem is asking for the remainder. *Maximum* and *at most* are clue phrases for dropping the remainder. *Minimum* and *at least* are clue phrases for rounding up to the next whole number.

Practice

Directions: For questions 1 through 5, find each answer. Then write whether you rounded the quotient to the next whole number, you dropped the remainder, or the remainder is the answer.

1. Marcy needs 5 buttons for each shirt. How many buttons will be left over?

_____

2. Steve has $82 to spend on lunches. He pays $5 each day for his lunch. How many days can Steve buy lunch?

_____

3. Mrs. O'Brien is planning a party for 86 people. Each table seats 6 people. How many tables will Mrs. O'Brien need for the party?

_____

4. Marco has 92 stickers. He is going to divide the stickers equally into 8 bags for party favors. How many extra stickers will Marco have?

_____

5. The members of an ecology club have 54 young pine trees to plant. They want to plant the trees throughout the city in groups of 7 trees. How many groups of 7 pine trees will the club be able to plant?

_____

Dividing by Multiples of 10 and 100

You can use division facts to solve problems that have a multiple of 10 or 100 as a factor. Remember, multiples of 10 include 10, 20, 30, and so on. Multiples of 100 include 100, 200, 300, and so on.

 **Example**

Use a division fact and a pattern of zeros to solve 2,100 ÷ 300.

21 ÷ 3 = 7

21**0** ÷ 3**0** = 7

2,1**00** ÷ 3**00** = 7

You can also use this rule: **Remove any zeros from the divisor. Remove the same number of zeros from the dividend. Then divide.**

Examples

2,4**00** ÷ 6**00** = 24 ÷ 6 = 4 (Remove two zeros from both the divisor and the dividend.)

5**00** ÷ 5**0** = 50 ÷ 5 = 10 (Remove one zero from both the divisor and the dividend.)

Practice

Directions: For questions 1 through 10, find the quotient

1. 30 ÷ 10 = _____

2. 240 ÷ 3 = _____

3. 4,200 ÷ 7 = _____

4. 180 ÷ 20 = _____

5. 200 ÷ 40 = _____

6. 400 ÷ 100 = _____

7. 2,500 ÷ 50 = _____

8. 2,800 ÷ 400 = _____

9. 4,800 ÷ 80 = _____

10. 700 ÷ 70 = _____

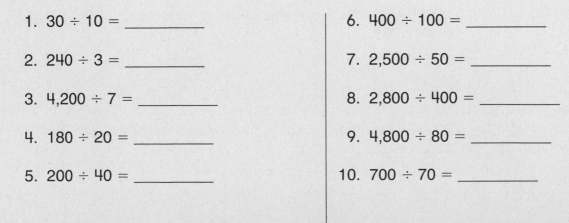

New York Math Practice begins on the following page.

New York Math Practice

1 Alicia wants to represent the number sentence 6 × 4 = 24. Which shows a way that she can use?

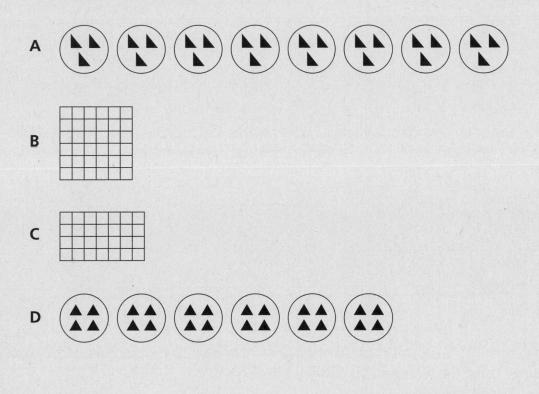

A

B

C

D

2 3,600 ÷ 40 =

A   9

B   90

C   900

D   9,000

3 While on a nature walk, Megan took 78 photos of birds. She put them in an album with 3 photos on each page. How many pages of the album did Megan use?

A 22

B 26

C 224

D 253

4 Saturday was a sunny day, and 5,374 people visited the park. It rained on Sunday, and only 956 people visited the park. How many park visitors were there on the weekend?

A 4,418

B 5,220

C 6,330

D 14,934

5 Carlos can fit 6 model cars on each shelf. He has 20 model cars. How many shelves does Carlos need to display all of his cars?

A 2

B 3

C 4

D 6

6 Which expression has the same value as $(4 \times 3) \times 2$?

A $4 + (3 + 2)$

B $4 + (3 \times 2)$

C $4 \times (3 + 2)$

D $4 \times (3 \times 2)$

7 Tyrell makes the table below about tall buildings in the United States.

BUILDINGS IN THE UNITED STATES

Building	Height (in feet)
Empire State Building, New York	1,250
John Hancock Center, Chicago	1,127
Key Tower, Cleveland	947

How much taller is the Empire State Building than the Key Tower?

A   123 feet

B   303 feet

C   317 feet

D   2,197 feet

8 $94 \div 7 =$

A   13 R3

B   14

C   14 R4

D   133

9 William is trying to solve 80×20. Which basic fact could he use?

A $8 \times 2 = 16$

B $8 \div 2 = 4$

C $8 \times 10 = 80$

D $10 \times 10 = 100$

10 23 × 3 =

A 66

B 69

C 79

D 96

11 Rosa and her friends blew up 63 balloons for a party. They are putting them in bunches of 5 balloons each. How many bunches of balloons can they make?

A 12

B 13

C 14

D 15

12 A wagon holds 98 bales of hay. There are 7 wagons. How many bales of hay are there?

A 686

B 756

C 806

D 6,356

13 Mr. Robinson planted 12 rows of tulip bulbs. There are 36 bulbs in each row. How many bulbs did Mr. Robinson plant?

A 3

B 24

C 48

D 432

14 Ana has a jar for pennies in her room. Last year, she collected 1,568 pennies. This year, she has already collected 1,347 pennies. Which is the total number of pennies that Ana has collected so far?

A 2,805

B 2,815

C 2,915

D 3,915

15 $74 \times 53 =$

A 362

B 592

C 2,922

D 3,922

16 Which multiplication fact could you use to solve $48 \div 8$?

A $5 \times 9 = 45$

B $6 \times 7 = 42$

C $6 \times 8 = 48$

D $7 \times 7 = 49$

17 A school has 14 buses. Each bus can hold 57 students. Kim says that the buses could hold a total of 795 students. Julie says that the buses could hold a total of 798 students. Without multiplying, determine which girl could be correct.

Answer _____

On the lines below, explain your thinking.

_____

_____

18 There are 24 students in Ms. Jeffer's class. She wants to divide them into 3 equal groups. She asks her class to find how many students she should put in each group.

Part A

Angelo used grouping to show 24 students divided into 3 equal groups. Show what Angelo's drawing might look like.

Part B

Stacey used repeated subtraction to show a way to divide 24 students into 3 equal groups. Show the work Stacey could have done.

Part C

How many students should Ms. Jeffers put in each group?

Answer _____ students

Performance Indicator: 4.N.7

Lesson 3: Fractions

A **fraction** is a number that names parts of a whole or parts of a group. The **numerator** of the fraction is the top number. It tells you how many parts of the whole or group you have. The **denominator** of the fraction is the bottom number. It tells you how many parts the whole is divided into or how many parts are in the group.

$\dfrac{2}{5}$ ← **numerator**
$\phantom{\dfrac{2}{5}}$ ← **denominator**

Understanding Fractions

Fractions can be shown on a number line. Fractions can also show division of whole numbers.

Fractions on Number Lines

Fractions shown on a number line can have any denominator. Watch to see how much the fractions on the number line increase each time.

Example

What fraction should replace the *x* on the number line?

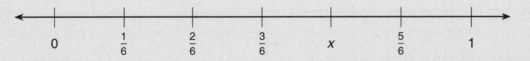

The fractions on the number line increase by $\frac{1}{6}$ each time. The *x* is between $\frac{3}{6}$ and $\frac{5}{6}$.

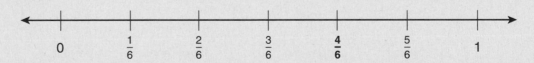

The fraction that should replace the *x* on the number line is $\frac{4}{6}$.

Example

Plot $\frac{1}{8}$, $\frac{2}{8}$, $\frac{4}{8}$, and $\frac{6}{8}$ on the number line.

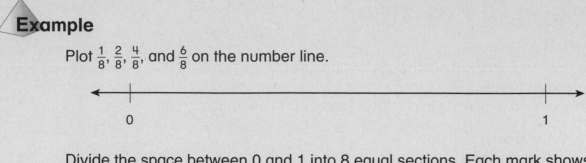

Divide the space between 0 and 1 into 8 equal sections. Each mark shows a fraction with a denominator of 8. The first mark shows where $\frac{1}{8}$ is, the second mark shows where $\frac{2}{8}$ is, and so on.

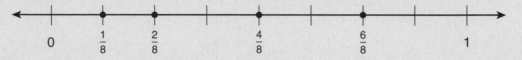

Fractions as Divisions of Whole Numbers

A fraction also represents the division of two whole numbers, with the numerator as the dividend and the denominator as the divisor. For example, $\frac{1}{4}$ would be "one divided by four."

Example

Four people are sharing 2 large sandwiches. Each sandwich is the same size, and each person gets the same amount. How much of a sandwich does each person get?

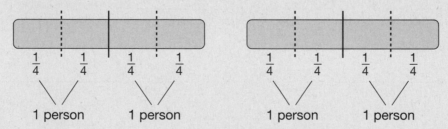

Each person gets 2 pieces of a sandwich. Each piece is $\frac{1}{4}$ of a sandwich. So, each person gets $\frac{2}{4}$ of a sandwich.

You can also solve this problem by thinking about division: 2 sandwiches divided by 4 people.

$$2 \div 4 = \frac{2}{4}$$

Each person will get $\frac{2}{4}$ of a sandwich.

 **Practice**

1. Plot $\frac{1}{5}$, $\frac{2}{5}$, $\frac{3}{5}$, and $\frac{4}{5}$ on the number line.

```
←——————|————————————————————————————————————|——→
        0                                      1
```

2. Plot $\frac{1}{10}$, $\frac{3}{10}$, $\frac{5}{10}$, and $\frac{9}{10}$ on the number line.

```
←——————|————————————————————————————————————|——→
        0                                      1
```

Directions: Use the number line to answer questions 3 through 5.

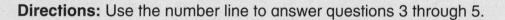
```
←——————|——————————|——————————|——————————|——————————|——→
        0          1/4                                1
                        ____        ____
```

3. Write in the missing fractions on the blanks under the number line.

4. What do the fractions increase by on the number line? _____

5. What is another way to write the 1 on the number line? _____

Directions: For questions 6 through 11, write each quotient as a fraction.

6. $1 \div 3 = $ _____   8. $7 \div 8 = $ _____

7. $4 \div 5 = $ _____   9. $6 \div 10 = $ _____

10. Three friends are sharing 2 apples. How much of an apple does each friend get? _____

11. Ten children are sharing 3 quarts of juice. How much juice does each child get? _____

Equivalent Fractions

Fractions that name the same amount are **equivalent fractions**. You can make a model or draw a picture to help you find equivalent fractions.

Example

Maria bought a piece of ribbon and give $\frac{2}{4}$ of it to her friend. Nadine bought the same length piece of ribbon and gave $\frac{1}{2}$ of it to her friend. Who has more ribbon remaining?

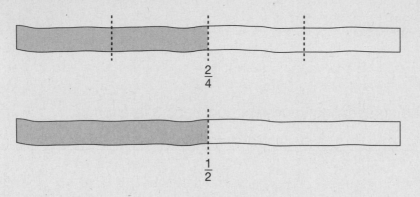

$$\frac{2}{4}$$

$$\frac{1}{2}$$

Maria and Nadine both have the same amount of ribbon remaining. The model shows that $\frac{2}{4}$ and $\frac{1}{2}$ are equivalent fractions.

Example

Use the fraction bars to find out if $\frac{1}{3}$ and $\frac{2}{6}$ are equivalent fractions.

1		
$\frac{1}{3}$	$\frac{1}{3}$	$\frac{1}{3}$
$\frac{1}{6}$ $\frac{1}{6}$	$\frac{1}{6}$ $\frac{1}{6}$	$\frac{1}{6}$ $\frac{1}{6}$

The bars for $\frac{1}{3}$ and $\frac{2}{6}$ are the same length. They show that $\frac{1}{3}$ and $\frac{2}{6}$ are equivalent fractions.

Example

Mario and Abby each had the same size pizza. Mario's pizza was cut into 6 slices and he ate 2 of those slices. Abby's pizza was cut into 3 slices and she ate 1 of those slices. Who had more pizza left?

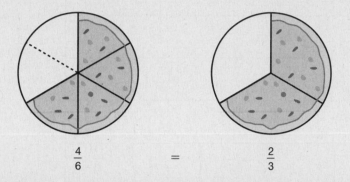

$$\frac{4}{6} \qquad = \qquad \frac{2}{3}$$

Mario and Abby both had the same amount of pizza left. The picture shows that $\frac{4}{6}$ and $\frac{2}{3}$ are equivalent fractions.

Example

Use the chart to find a fraction that is equivalent to $\frac{1}{2}$.

$\frac{1}{2}$					$\frac{1}{2}$				
$\frac{1}{3}$			$\frac{1}{3}$			$\frac{1}{3}$			
$\frac{1}{4}$		$\frac{1}{4}$		$\frac{1}{4}$		$\frac{1}{4}$			
$\frac{1}{5}$		$\frac{1}{5}$		$\frac{1}{5}$		$\frac{1}{5}$		$\frac{1}{5}$	
$\frac{1}{6}$		$\frac{1}{6}$		$\frac{1}{6}$		$\frac{1}{6}$		$\frac{1}{6}$	$\frac{1}{6}$
$\frac{1}{10}$	$\frac{1}{10}$	$\frac{1}{10}$	$\frac{1}{10}$	$\frac{1}{10}$	$\frac{1}{10}$	$\frac{1}{10}$	$\frac{1}{10}$	$\frac{1}{10}$	$\frac{1}{10}$

The fraction $\frac{2}{4}$ is equivalent to $\frac{1}{2}$.

If you look further down the chart, you can see that $\frac{3}{6}$ and $\frac{5}{10}$ are also equivalent to $\frac{1}{2}$.

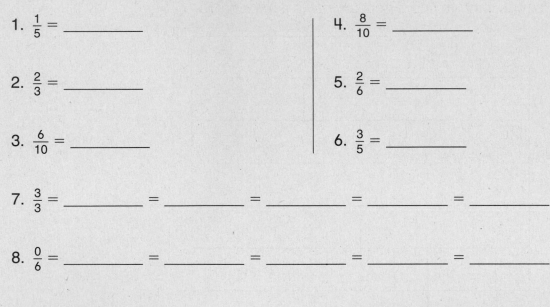

Practice

Directions: Use the following chart to answer questions 1 through 9.

1. $\frac{1}{5}$ = _____

2. $\frac{2}{3}$ = _____

3. $\frac{6}{10}$ = _____

4. $\frac{8}{10}$ = _____

5. $\frac{2}{6}$ = _____

6. $\frac{3}{5}$ = _____

7. $\frac{3}{3}$ = _____ = _____ = _____ = _____ = _____

8. $\frac{0}{6}$ = _____ = _____ = _____ = _____ = _____

9. What fractions in the chart do **not** have any equivalent fractions showing?

_____

Directions: For questions 10 through 13, shade an equivalent fraction to the figure shown. Then write the equivalent fractions.

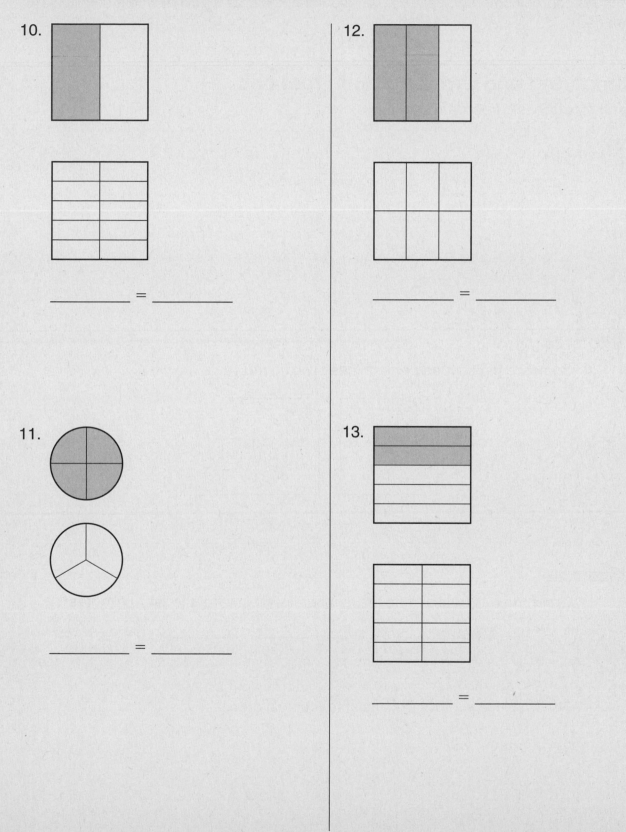

10.

_____ = _____

11.

_____ = _____

12.

_____ = _____

13.

_____ = _____

Comparing and Ordering Fractions

Fractions can be compared using $<$, $>$, and $=$ in the same way that whole numbers are compared.

Comparing and Ordering Unit Fractions

A **unit fraction** is a fraction with a numerator of 1.

Example

Compare the fractions on the number line below.

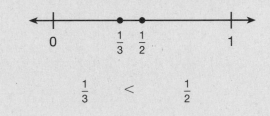

$$\frac{1}{3} \quad < \quad \frac{1}{2}$$

Example

Compare the shaded parts of these two figures.

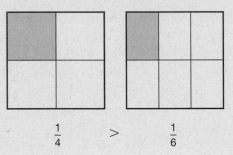

$$\frac{1}{4} \quad > \quad \frac{1}{6}$$

Example

Order the unit fractions on the number line below from **least** to **greatest**.

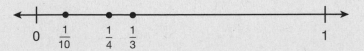

The fractions in order from least to greatest are $\frac{1}{10}, \frac{1}{4}, \frac{1}{3}$.

Performance Indicators: 3.N.15, 4.N.9, 4.A.2

Comparing and Ordering Fractions with the Same Denominator

When fractions have **like denominators,** compare their numerators. The fraction with the **larger numerator** is the **larger fraction**.

Example

Compare the shaded parts of these two figures.

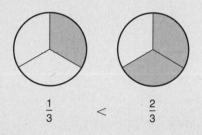

$$\frac{1}{3} \quad < \quad \frac{2}{3}$$

Example

Use the number line to compare $\frac{5}{6}$ and $\frac{3}{6}$.

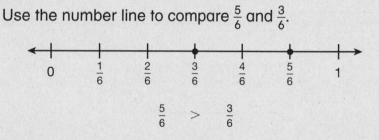

$$\frac{5}{6} \quad > \quad \frac{3}{6}$$

Example

Use the number line to order $\frac{3}{5}$, $\frac{1}{5}$, and $\frac{4}{5}$ from **greatest** to **least**.

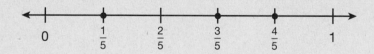

The fractions in order from greatest to least are $\frac{4}{5}$, $\frac{3}{5}$, $\frac{1}{5}$.

Practice

Directions: For questions 1 through 5, write the fraction represented by the shaded part(s) of each figure. Then use <, >, or = to compare the fractions.

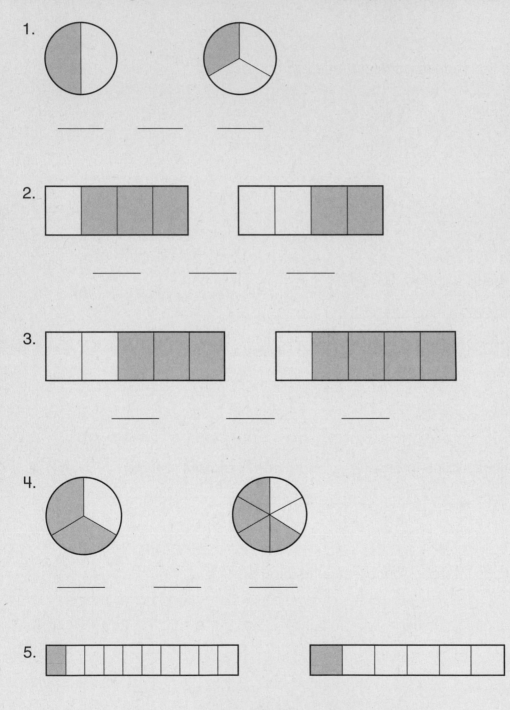

1.

_____ _____ _____

2.

_____ _____ _____

3.

_____ _____ _____

4.

_____ _____ _____

5.

_____ _____ _____

Performance Indicators: 3.N.15, 4.N.9, 4.A.2

Directions: For questions 6 through 9, show the approximate locations of the given fractions on the number lines. Then, compare the fractions.

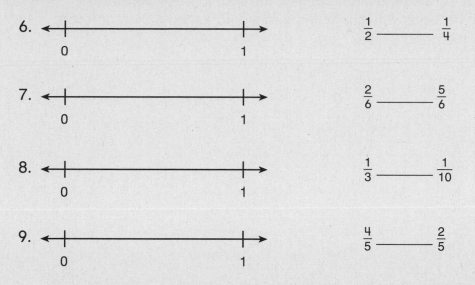

6.

$\dfrac{1}{2}$ —————— $\dfrac{1}{4}$

7.

$\dfrac{2}{6}$ —————— $\dfrac{5}{6}$

8.

$\dfrac{1}{3}$ —————— $\dfrac{1}{10}$

9.

$\dfrac{4}{5}$ —————— $\dfrac{2}{5}$

10. Show the approximate locations of $\dfrac{1}{5}$, $\dfrac{1}{2}$, and $\dfrac{1}{3}$ on the number line below. Then write the fractions in order from **greatest** to **least**.

_____

11. Show the approximate locations of $\dfrac{6}{10}$, $\dfrac{1}{10}$, and $\dfrac{8}{10}$ on the number line below. Then write the fractions in order from **least** to **greatest**.

_____

Adding Fractions

When fractions have the same denominators, they are said to have **common denominators**. To add fractions with common denominators, add the numerators and write the sum over the denominator.

Example

Add: $\frac{7}{10} + \frac{1}{10}$

$$\frac{7+1}{10} = \frac{8}{10}$$

$$\frac{7}{10} + \frac{1}{10} = \frac{\mathbf{8}}{\mathbf{10}}$$

Example

Andrew has completed $\frac{3}{8}$ of his homework. He completed $\frac{4}{8}$ more of his homework before dinner. How much of his homework has Andrew completed?

Add $\frac{3}{8}$ and $\frac{4}{8}$.

$$\frac{3}{8} + \frac{4}{8} = \frac{3+4}{8}$$

$$= \frac{7}{8}$$

$$\frac{3}{8} + \frac{4}{8} = \frac{\mathbf{7}}{\mathbf{8}}$$

Andrew has completed $\frac{7}{8}$ of his homework.

Practice

Directions: For questions 1 through 12, add.

1. $\frac{1}{10} + \frac{5}{10} =$ _____

2. $\frac{3}{8} + \frac{2}{8} =$ _____

3. $\frac{1}{8} + \frac{2}{8} =$ _____

4. $\frac{1}{4} + \frac{1}{4} =$ _____

Performance Indicator: 4.N.23

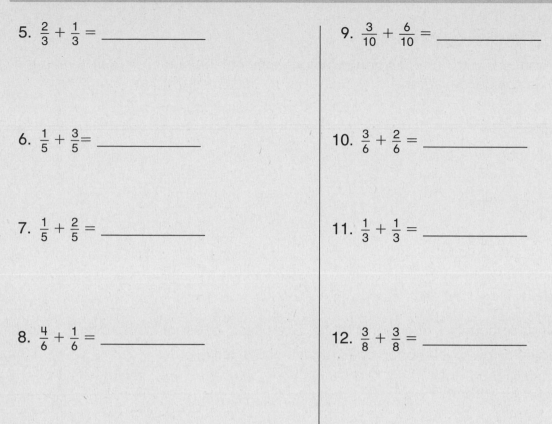

5. $\frac{2}{3} + \frac{1}{3} =$ _____

6. $\frac{1}{5} + \frac{3}{5} =$ _____

7. $\frac{1}{5} + \frac{2}{5} =$ _____

8. $\frac{4}{6} + \frac{1}{6} =$ _____

9. $\frac{3}{10} + \frac{6}{10} =$ _____

10. $\frac{3}{6} + \frac{2}{6} =$ _____

11. $\frac{1}{3} + \frac{1}{3} =$ _____

12. $\frac{3}{8} + \frac{3}{8} =$ _____

13. Eric jogged for $\frac{1}{4}$ of an hour and biked for $\frac{2}{4}$ of an hour. How long did Eric jog and bike altogether?

_____

14. Brandon ate $\frac{3}{8}$ of a pizza, and Linda ate $\frac{1}{8}$ of a pizza. How much pizza did Brandon and Linda eat altogether?

_____

15. Marty hiked $\frac{5}{10}$ of a mile before lunch and $\frac{3}{10}$ of a mile after lunch. How far did Marty hike altogether?

_____

16. Callie read $\frac{1}{6}$ of her book on Saturday. She read another $\frac{3}{6}$ of her book on Sunday. How much of the book has Callie read so far?

_____

Subtracting Fractions

To subtract fractions with common denominators, subtract the numerators and write the difference over the denominator.

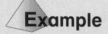 **Example**

Subtract: $\frac{4}{5} - \frac{1}{5}$

$$\frac{4-1}{5} = \frac{3}{5}$$

$$\frac{4}{5} - \frac{1}{5} = \mathbf{\frac{3}{5}}$$

Example

Amanda bought $\frac{7}{8}$ of a foot of fabric. She uses $\frac{3}{8}$ of a foot of fabric for a school project. How much ribbon does Amanda have left?

Subtract $\frac{3}{8}$ from $\frac{7}{8}$.

$$\frac{7}{8} - \frac{3}{8} = \frac{7-3}{8}$$

$$= \frac{4}{8}$$

$$\frac{7}{8} - \frac{3}{8} = \mathbf{\frac{4}{8}}$$

Amanda has $\frac{4}{8}$ of a foot of fabric left.

Practice

Directions: For questions 1 through 12, subtract.

1. $\frac{2}{3} - \frac{1}{3} =$ _____

2. $\frac{4}{5} - \frac{3}{5} =$ _____

3. $\frac{5}{6} - \frac{4}{6} =$ _____

4. $\frac{3}{4} - \frac{1}{4} =$ _____

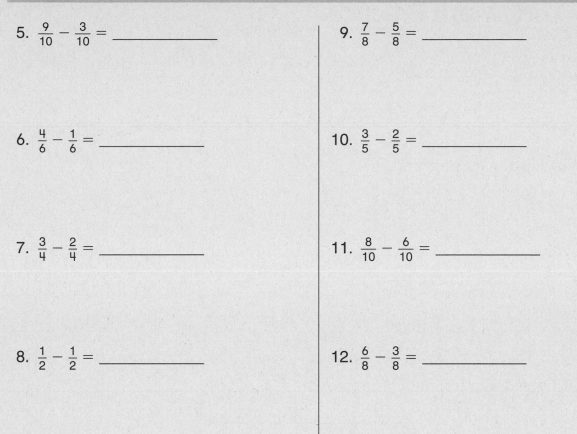

5. $\frac{9}{10} - \frac{3}{10} =$ _____

6. $\frac{4}{6} - \frac{1}{6} =$ _____

7. $\frac{3}{4} - \frac{2}{4} =$ _____

8. $\frac{1}{2} - \frac{1}{2} =$ _____

9. $\frac{7}{8} - \frac{5}{8} =$ _____

10. $\frac{3}{5} - \frac{2}{5} =$ _____

11. $\frac{8}{10} - \frac{6}{10} =$ _____

12. $\frac{6}{8} - \frac{3}{8} =$ _____

13. Carla's gas tank was $\frac{2}{3}$ full. After she drove to Albany, her gas tank was $\frac{1}{3}$ full. What fraction of a tank of gas did Carla use to drive to Albany?

_____

14. Christopher was at the beach collecting seashells. He filled up his bucket $\frac{3}{4}$ of the way with seashells. He shared $\frac{1}{4}$ of the bucket of shells with his brother. How full was his bucket with seashells then?

_____

15. Sebastian plans to run $\frac{7}{8}$ of a mile. He ran $\frac{3}{8}$ of the mile before he stopped for a break. How much of a mile does Sebastian have left to run?

_____

16. Stephanie had $\frac{9}{10}$ of her granola bar left over. She shared $\frac{3}{10}$ of it with her friend Charleigh. How much of her granola bar does Stephanie have left?

_____

New York Math Practice

1   Ahmad drew this number line.

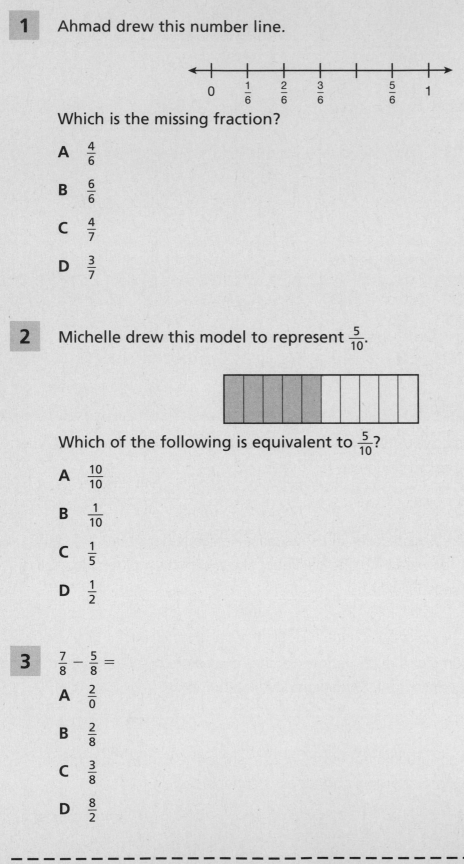

Which is the missing fraction?

A $\frac{4}{6}$

B $\frac{6}{6}$

C $\frac{4}{7}$

D $\frac{3}{7}$

2   Michelle drew this model to represent $\frac{5}{10}$.

Which of the following is equivalent to $\frac{5}{10}$?

A $\frac{10}{10}$

B $\frac{1}{10}$

C $\frac{1}{5}$

D $\frac{1}{2}$

3 $\frac{7}{8} - \frac{5}{8} =$

A $\frac{2}{0}$

B $\frac{2}{8}$

C $\frac{3}{8}$

D $\frac{8}{2}$

4 Use the figures below.

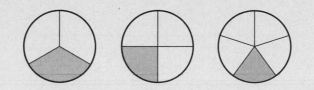

Which statement correctly compares the shaded parts of the figures?

A $\frac{1}{3} > \frac{1}{4}$

B $\frac{1}{3} < \frac{1}{5}$

C $\frac{1}{4} > \frac{1}{3}$

D $\frac{1}{4} < \frac{1}{5}$

5 Use the figure below.

$\frac{1}{2}$		$\frac{1}{2}$	
$\frac{1}{3}$	$\frac{1}{3}$	$\frac{1}{3}$	

$\frac{1}{4}$	$\frac{1}{4}$	$\frac{1}{4}$	$\frac{1}{4}$
$\frac{1}{5}$	$\frac{1}{5}$	$\frac{1}{5}$	$\frac{1}{5}$	$\frac{1}{5}$

Which list is in order from **greatest** to **least**?

A $\frac{1}{2}, \frac{1}{3}, \frac{1}{4}, \frac{1}{5}$

B $\frac{1}{2}, \frac{1}{4}, \frac{1}{3}, \frac{1}{5}$

C $\frac{1}{5}, \frac{1}{3}, \frac{1}{4}, \frac{1}{2}$

D $\frac{1}{5}, \frac{1}{4}, \frac{1}{3}, \frac{1}{2}$

6 Which fraction is represented by A on the number line?

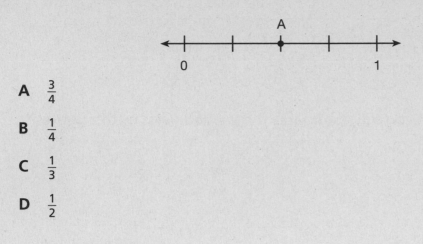

A $\frac{3}{4}$

B $\frac{1}{4}$

C $\frac{1}{3}$

D $\frac{1}{2}$

7 Van drew these fraction models.

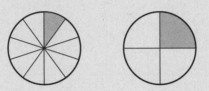

Which statement correctly compares the fractions?

A $\frac{1}{4} < \frac{1}{10}$

B $\frac{1}{4} = \frac{1}{10}$

C $\frac{1}{10} < \frac{1}{4}$

D $\frac{1}{10} > \frac{1}{4}$

8 Five friends are sharing 3 oranges equally. How much of an orange does each friend get?

A $\frac{2}{3}$

B $\frac{5}{3}$

C $\frac{3}{5}$

D $\frac{3}{8}$

9 Use the figure below.

$\frac{1}{2}$		$\frac{1}{2}$	
$\frac{1}{3}$	$\frac{1}{3}$	$\frac{1}{3}$	
$\frac{1}{4}$	$\frac{1}{4}$	$\frac{1}{4}$	$\frac{1}{4}$
$\frac{1}{5}$	$\frac{1}{5}$	$\frac{1}{5}$	$\frac{1}{5}$ $\frac{1}{5}$
$\frac{1}{6}$ $\frac{1}{6}$	$\frac{1}{6}$ $\frac{1}{6}$	$\frac{1}{6}$ $\frac{1}{6}$	
$\frac{1}{10}$ $\frac{1}{10}$ $\frac{1}{10}$ $\frac{1}{10}$ $\frac{1}{10}$ $\frac{1}{10}$ $\frac{1}{10}$ $\frac{1}{10}$ $\frac{1}{10}$ $\frac{1}{10}$			

Which pair names equivalent fractions?

A $\frac{2}{3}$ and $\frac{3}{5}$

B $\frac{4}{6}$ and $\frac{2}{3}$

C $\frac{1}{4}$ and $\frac{2}{6}$

D $\frac{4}{10}$ and $\frac{1}{2}$

10 Christina drank $\frac{2}{8}$ of a cup of juice for breakfast. She drank $\frac{4}{8}$ of a cup of juice for lunch. How much of a cup of juice did Christina drink in all?

A $\frac{8}{6}$

B $\frac{2}{8}$

C $\frac{6}{8}$

D $\frac{6}{16}$

11 Which list is in order from **least** to **greatest**?

A $\frac{2}{10}, \frac{6}{10}, \frac{5}{10}$

B $\frac{2}{10}, \frac{5}{10}, \frac{6}{10}$

C $\frac{5}{10}, \frac{2}{10}, \frac{6}{10}$

D $\frac{6}{10}, \frac{5}{10}, \frac{2}{10}$

12 Look at the number line.

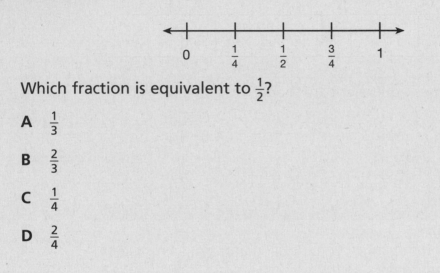

Which fraction is equivalent to $\frac{1}{2}$?

A $\frac{1}{3}$

B $\frac{2}{3}$

C $\frac{1}{4}$

D $\frac{2}{4}$

13 Amanda bought some peaches. She used $\frac{3}{6}$ of the peaches in a fruit salad and $\frac{1}{6}$ of the peaches to make a fruit smoothie. What fraction of the peaches has Amanda used?

Show your work.

Answer _____ of the peaches

Performance Indicators: 4.N.10, 4.N.11

Lesson 4: Decimals

A **decimal** expresses a whole divided into ten equal parts (ten**ths**), into one hundred equal parts (hundred**ths**), and so on.

Reading and Writing Decimals

You can write a decimal using digits, words, or models.

Digits and Words

0, 1, 2, 3, 4, 5, 6, 7, 8, and 9 are the digits used to write decimals.

The decimal 0.24 is written in standard form. A **decimal point** is used to separate the whole-number part of the decimal from the part that is less than 1.

In word form, the decimal 0.24 is written *twenty-four hundredths*. You read the number to the right of the decimal point as a whole number, followed by the last digit's place value.

Models

Decimals can be shown using models.

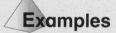

Examples

This model shows 0.6.

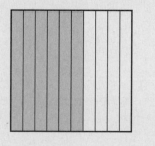

This model shows 0.24.

Place Value

Place-value tables show the value of the digits in a decimal.

Example

This place-value table shows the values of the digits of 0.24.

Ones	Decimal Point	Tenths	Hundredths
0	.	2	4

The digit 0 is in the ones place because there are no ones in this number.

The digit 2 is in the tenths place. Its value is 2 tenths or 0.2.

The digit 4 is in the hundredths place. Its value is 4 hundredths or 0.04.

Example

This place-value table shows the values of the digits of 0.08.

Ones	Decimal Point	Tenths	Hundredths
0	.	0	8

The digit 0 is in the ones place and the tenths place because there are no ones and no tenths in this number.

The digit 8 is in the hundredths place. Its value is 8 hundredths or 0.08.

This decimal is read *eight hundredths*.

Money

Money amounts are written as decimals. Even though money amounts are read as dollars and cents, the cents represent tenths and hundredths.

Example

This place value table shows the money amount $0.36 or 36 cents.

	Ones	Decimal Point	Tenths	Hundredths
$	0	.	3	6

Practice

Directions: For questions 1 through 4, shade in the correct number of parts to show the decimals.

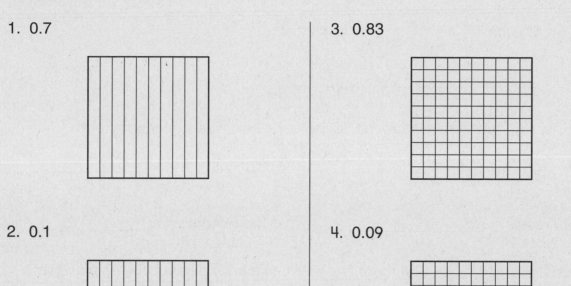

1. 0.7

3. 0.83

2. 0.1

4. 0.09

Directions: For questions 5 and 6, write the decimal that describes the part of the grid that is shaded.

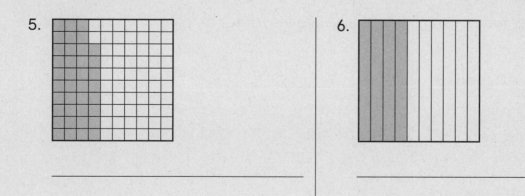

5.

6.

Directions: For questions 7 through 9, write the decimals in word form.

7. 0.03 _____

8. 0.27 _____

9. 0.5 _____

Directions: For questions 10 through 13, write the decimals in standard form.

10. forty-eight hundredths _____

11. three tenths _____

12. eighty hundredths _____

13. two hundredths _____

Directions: For questions 14 through 16, write the money amounts in the place-value table.

14. $0.70

15. $0.59

16. $0.06

	Ones	Decimal Point	Tenths	Hundredths
$		•		
$		•		
$		•		

Directions: For questions 17 through 20, write the money amounts using decimals.

17. 2 dimes and 8 pennies _____

18. 3 dimes _____

19. 2 quarters and 4 pennies _____

20. 13 nickels _____

Performance Indicators: 4.N.12, 4.A.2

Comparing and Ordering Decimals

One way to compare and order decimals is to think about money.

Example

Compare $0.32 and $0.38

$0.32 and $0.38 have the same number of dimes.

$0.32 has fewer pennies than $0.38.

So, $0.32 < $0.38.

You can also use dimes and pennies to model decimal amounts that are not money amounts. There are 10 dimes in a whole dollar, so think of dimes as tenths. There are 100 pennies in a whole dollar, so think of pennies as hundredths.

Example

Compare 0.57 and 0.2.

The model for 0.57 has 5 dimes.

The model for 0.2 has 2 dimes.

Five dimes have a greater value than 2 dimes.

So, 0.57 > 0.2.

Example

Order $0.46, $0.53, and $0.50 from **least** to **greatest**.

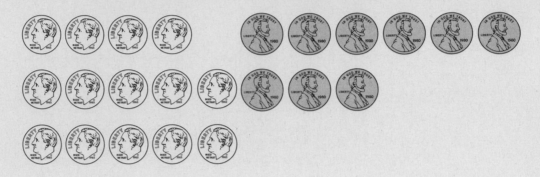

$0.46 has the least number of dimes.

So, $0.46 has the least value.

$0.53 and $0.50 have the same number of dimes.

$0.53 has a greater number of pennies than $0.50.

So, $0.53 is greater than $0.50.

The order from **least** to **greatest** is $0.46, $0.50, $0.53.

Decimals can also be compared and ordered using a number line.

Example

Order 0.38, 0.3, and 0.56 from **greatest** to **least**.

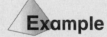

The order from **greatest** to **least** is 0.56, 0.38, 0.3.

Performance Indicators: 4.N.12, 4.A.2

Practice

Directions: For questions 1 through 10, compare the decimals. Write >, <, or =.

1. $0.56 ___=___ $0.56

2. 0.88 ___>___ 0.86

3. 0.03 ___>___ 0.3
   $\frac{3}{100}$ $\frac{3}{10}$

4. $0.64 ___>___ $0.40

5. 0.27 ___=___ 0.27

6. 0.5 ___<___ 0.15

7. 0.94 ___<___ 0.96

8. $0.08 ___<___ $0.80 $\frac{80}{100}$
   $\frac{8}{100}$

9. 0.2 ___<___ 0.20

10. 0.50 ___<___ 0.51

11. Plot the following decimals on the number line. Then, write the decimals in order from **least** to **greatest**.

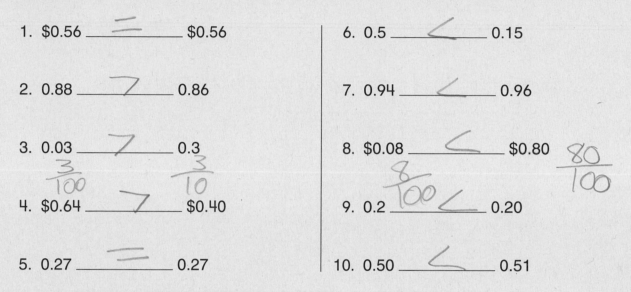

0.4   0.04 $\frac{4}{100}$ 0.93 $\frac{93}{100}$

$\frac{4}{10}$

0   0.1   0.2   0.3   0.4   0.5   0.6   0.7   0.8   0.9   1

0.4, 0.04, 0.93

Directions: Use the following information to answer questions 12 and 13.

The following are the amounts of change Sam and his friends have in their pockets.

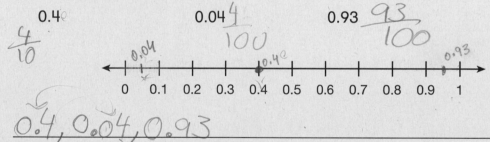

Sam: $0.80   Steve: $0.67   Ben: $0.91   Carl: $0.76
     $\frac{}{100}$ $\frac{}{100}$ $\frac{}{100}$ $\frac{}{100}$

12. Who has the **least** amount of change in his pocket?

   A. Sam

   B. Steve

   C. Ben

   D. Carl

13. Who has the **greatest** amount of change in his pocket?

   A. Sam

   B. Steve

   C. Ben

   D. Carl

Adding Decimals

You can use a hundreds chart to add decimals.

Example

Add: 0.34 + 0.18

Start by shading 0.34 of the hundreds chart (34 of the 100 squares).

1	2	3	4	5	6	7	8	9	10
11	12	13	14	15	16	17	18	19	20
21	22	23	24	25	26	27	28	29	30
31	32	33	34	35	36	37	38	39	40
41	42	43	44	45	46	47	48	49	50
51	52	53	54	55	56	57	58	59	60
61	62	63	64	65	66	67	68	69	70
71	72	73	74	75	76	77	78	79	80
81	82	83	84	85	86	87	88	89	90
91	92	93	94	95	96	97	98	99	100

Add 0.18 by shading the next 18 squares on the chart.

1	2	3	4	5	6	7	8	9	10
11	12	13	14	15	16	17	18	19	20
21	22	23	24	25	26	27	28	29	30
31	32	33	34	35	36	37	38	39	40
41	42	43	44	45	46	47	48	49	50
51	52	53	54	55	56	57	58	59	60
61	62	63	64	65	66	67	68	69	70
71	72	73	74	75	76	77	78	79	80
81	82	83	84	85	86	87	88	89	90
91	92	93	94	95	96	97	98	99	100

A total of 52 squares are shaded. Therefore, 0.34 + 0.18 = 0.52.

Money amounts can be added in the same way decimals are added. Remember that cents are hundredths of a dollar.

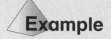

Example

Add: $0.29 + $0.43

$0.29 is 29 hundredths of a dollar. So, start by shading 0.29 of the hundreds chart.

1	2	3	4	5	6	7	8	9	10
11	12	13	14	15	16	17	18	19	20
21	22	23	24	25	26	27	28	29	30
31	32	33	34	35	36	37	38	39	40
41	42	43	44	45	46	47	48	49	50
51	52	53	54	55	56	57	58	59	60
61	62	63	64	65	66	67	68	69	70
71	72	73	74	75	76	77	78	79	80
81	82	83	84	85	86	87	88	89	90
91	92	93	94	95	96	97	98	99	100

$0.43 is 43 hundredths of a dollar. Add 0.43 by shading the next 43 squares on the chart.

1	2	3	4	5	6	7	8	9	10
11	12	13	14	15	16	17	18	19	20
21	22	23	24	25	26	27	28	29	30
31	32	33	34	35	36	37	38	39	40
41	42	43	44	45	46	47	48	49	50
51	52	53	54	55	56	57	58	59	60
61	62	63	64	65	66	67	68	69	70
71	72	73	74	75	76	77	78	79	80
81	82	83	84	85	86	87	88	89	90
91	92	93	94	95	96	97	98	99	100

A total of 72 squares are shaded. Therefore, $0.29 + $0.43 = $0.72.

Practice

Directions: For questions 1 through 8, add. Shade the hundreds charts to help you.

1. 0.47 + 0.32 = _0.79_

$$\begin{array}{r} 4\overset{1}{7} \\ +\ 32 \\ \hline 79 \end{array}$$

1	2	3	4	5	6	7	8	9	10
11	12	13	14	15	16	17	18	19	20
21	22	23	24	25	26	27	28	29	30
31	32	33	34	35	36	37	38	39	40
41	42	43	44	45	46	47	48	49	50
51	52	53	54	55	56	57	58	59	60
61	62	63	64	65	66	67	68	69	70
71	72	73	74	75	76	77	78	79	80
81	82	83	84	85	86	87	88	89	90
91	92	93	94	95	96	97	98	99	100

3. 0.14 + 0.09 = _0.23_

$$\begin{array}{r} \overset{1}{1}4 \\ +\ 9 \\ \hline 23 \end{array}$$

1	2	3	4	5	6	7	8	9	10
11	12	13	14	15	16	17	18	19	20
21	22	23	24	25	26	27	28	29	30
31	32	33	34	35	36	37	38	39	40
41	42	43	44	45	46	47	48	49	50
51	52	53	54	55	56	57	58	59	60
61	62	63	64	65	66	67	68	69	70
71	72	73	74	75	76	77	78	79	80
81	82	83	84	85	86	87	88	89	90
91	92	93	94	95	96	97	98	99	100

2. 0.53 + 0.30 = _0.83_

1	2	3	4	5	6	7	8	9	10
11	12	13	14	15	16	17	18	19	20
21	22	23	24	25	26	27	28	29	30
31	32	33	34	35	36	37	38	39	40
41	42	43	44	45	46	47	48	49	50
51	52	53	54	55	56	57	58	59	60
61	62	63	64	65	66	67	68	69	70
71	72	73	74	75	76	77	78	79	80
81	82	83	84	85	86	87	88	89	90
91	92	93	94	95	96	97	98	99	100

4. $0.75 + $0.17 = _$0.99_

1	2	3	4	5	6	7	8	9	10
11	12	13	14	15	16	17	18	19	20
21	22	23	24	25	26	27	28	29	30
31	32	33	34	35	36	37	38	39	40
41	42	43	44	45	46	47	48	49	50
51	52	53	54	55	56	57	58	59	60
61	62	63	64	65	66	67	68	69	70
71	72	73	74	75	76	77	78	79	80
81	82	83	84	85	86	87	88	89	90
91	92	93	94	95	96	97	98	99	100

$$\begin{array}{r} 53 \\ +\ 30 \\ \hline 83 \end{array}$$

$$\begin{array}{r} \overset{1}{7}5 \\ +\ 17 \\ \hline 92 \end{array}$$

5. On Saturday, Kingston receives 0.25 inch of rain. On Sunday, it receives 0.48 inch of rain. How much rain does Kingston receive over the weekend?

_____

1	2	3	4	5	6	7	8	9	10
11	12	13	14	15	16	17	18	19	20
21	22	23	24	25	26	27	28	29	30
31	32	33	34	35	36	37	38	39	40
41	42	43	44	45	46	47	48	49	50
51	52	53	54	55	56	57	58	59	60
61	62	63	64	65	66	67	68	69	70
71	72	73	74	75	76	77	78	79	80
81	82	83	84	85	86	87	88	89	90
91	92	93	94	95	96	97	98	99	100

6. Enrique buys 0.36 pound of cashews and 0.54 pound of peanuts. What is the total weight of nuts Enrique buys?

_____

1	2	3	4	5	6	7	8	9	10
11	12	13	14	15	16	17	18	19	20
21	22	23	24	25	26	27	28	29	30
31	32	33	34	35	36	37	38	39	40
41	42	43	44	45	46	47	48	49	50
51	52	53	54	55	56	57	58	59	60
61	62	63	64	65	66	67	68	69	70
71	72	73	74	75	76	77	78	79	80
81	82	83	84	85	86	87	88	89	90
91	92	93	94	95	96	97	98	99	100

7. Mai has $0.45 in her pocket. She finds $0.26 on the sidewalk and picks it up. How much money does Mai have now?

_____

1	2	3	4	5	6	7	8	9	10
11	12	13	14	15	16	17	18	19	20
21	22	23	24	25	26	27	28	29	30
31	32	33	34	35	36	37	38	39	40
41	42	43	44	45	46	47	48	49	50
51	52	53	54	55	56	57	58	59	60
61	62	63	64	65	66	67	68	69	70
71	72	73	74	75	76	77	78	79	80
81	82	83	84	85	86	87	88	89	90
91	92	93	94	95	96	97	98	99	100

8. Kira buys a pencil for $0.39 and an eraser for $0.55. How much does Kira spend in all?

_____

1	2	3	4	5	6	7	8	9	10
11	12	13	14	15	16	17	18	19	20
21	22	23	24	25	26	27	28	29	30
31	32	33	34	35	36	37	38	39	40
41	42	43	44	45	46	47	48	49	50
51	52	53	54	55	56	57	58	59	60
61	62	63	64	65	66	67	68	69	70
71	72	73	74	75	76	77	78	79	80
81	82	83	84	85	86	87	88	89	90
91	92	93	94	95	96	97	98	99	100

Subtracting Decimals

You can also use a hundreds chart to subtract decimals.

⊿ **Example**

Subtract: 0.72 − 0.29

Start by shading 0.72 of the hundreds chart (72 of the 100 squares).

1	2	3	4	5	6	7	8	9	10
11	12	13	14	15	16	17	18	19	20
21	22	23	24	25	26	27	28	29	30
31	32	33	34	35	36	37	38	39	40
41	42	43	44	45	46	47	48	49	50
51	52	53	54	55	56	57	58	59	60
61	62	63	64	65	66	67	68	69	70
71	72	73	74	75	76	77	78	79	80
81	82	83	84	85	86	87	88	89	90
91	92	93	94	95	96	97	98	99	100

Subtract 0.29 by crossing out 29 of the shaded squares.

1	2	3	4	5	6	7	8	9	10
11	12	13	14	15	16	17	18	19	20
21	22	23	24	25	26	27	28	29	30
31	32	33	34	35	36	37	38	39	40
41	42	43	44	45	46	47	48	49	50
51	52	53	54	55	56	57	58	59	60
61	62	63	64	65	66	67	68	69	70
71	72	73	74	75	76	77	78	79	80
81	82	83	84	85	86	87	88	89	90
91	92	93	94	95	96	97	98	99	100

Of the shaded squares, 43 remain. Therefore, 0.72 − 0.29 = 0.43.

You can subtract money amounts in the same way you subtract decimals.

Example

Subtract: $0.53 − $0.39

$0.53 is 53 hundredths of a dollar. So, start by shading 0.53 of the hundreds chart.

1	2	3	4	5	6	7	8	9	10
11	12	13	14	15	16	17	18	19	20
21	22	23	24	25	26	27	28	29	30
31	32	33	34	35	36	37	38	39	40
41	42	43	44	45	46	47	48	49	50
51	52	53	54	55	56	57	58	59	60
61	62	63	64	65	66	67	68	69	70
71	72	73	74	75	76	77	78	79	80
81	82	83	84	85	86	87	88	89	90
91	92	93	94	95	96	97	98	99	100

$0.39 is 39 hundredths of a dollar. Subtract 0.39 by crossing out 39 of the shaded squares on the chart.

1	2	3	4	5	6	7	8	9	10
11	12	13	14	15	16	17	18	19	20
21	22	23	24	25	26	27	28	29	30
31	32	33	34	35	36	37	38	39	40
41	42	43	44	45	46	47	48	49	50
51	52	53	54	55	56	57	58	59	60
61	62	63	64	65	66	67	68	69	70
71	72	73	74	75	76	77	78	79	80
81	82	83	84	85	86	87	88	89	90
91	92	93	94	95	96	97	98	99	100

Of the shaded squares, 14 remain. Therefore, $0.53 − $0.39 = $0.14.

Practice

Directions: For questions 1 through 8, subtract. Use the hundreds charts to help you.

1. 0.45 − 0.27 = __0.18__   3 4 5 15
                              − 2 7
                              ─────
                               1 8
                              1 0 0

1	2	3	4	5	6	7	8	9	10
11	12	13	14	15	16	17	18	19	20
21	22	23	24	25	26	27	28	29	30
31	32	33	34	35	36	37	38	39	40
41	42	43	44	45	46	47	48	49	50
51	52	53	54	55	56	57	58	59	60
61	62	63	64	65	66	67	68	69	70
71	72	73	74	75	76	77	78	79	80
81	82	83	84	85	86	87	88	89	90
91	92	93	94	95	96	97	98	99	100

3. 0.36 − 0.08 = __0.28__   2 3 6 16
                             −   8
                             ──────
                             2 8

1	2	3	4	5	6	7	8	9	10
11	12	13	14	15	16	17	18	19	20
21	22	23	24	25	26	27	28	29	30
31	32	33	34	35	36	37	38	39	40
41	42	43	44	45	46	47	48	49	50
51	52	53	54	55	56	57	58	59	60
61	62	63	64	65	66	67	68	69	70
71	72	73	74	75	76	77	78	79	80
81	82	83	84	85	86	87	88	89	90
91	92	93	94	95	96	97	98	99	100

2. 0.60 − 0.34 = __0.26__

5 6 0 10
− 3 4
─────
2 6

1	2	3	4	5	6	7	8	9	10
11	12	13	14	15	16	17	18	19	20
21	22	23	24	25	26	27	28	29	30
31	32	33	34	35	36	37	38	39	40
41	42	43	44	45	46	47	48	49	50
51	52	53	54	55	56	57	58	59	60
61	62	63	64	65	66	67	68	69	70
71	72	73	74	75	76	77	78	79	80
81	82	83	84	85	86	87	88	89	90
91	92	93	94	95	96	97	98	99	100

4. $0.67 − $0.48 = __$0.19__

1	2	3	4	5	6	7	8	9	10
11	12	13	14	15	16	17	18	19	20
21	22	23	24	25	26	27	28	29	30
31	32	33	34	35	36	37	38	39	40
41	42	43	44	45	46	47	48	49	50
51	52	53	54	55	56	57	58	59	60
61	62	63	64	65	66	67	68	69	70
71	72	73	74	75	76	77	78	79	80
81	82	83	84	85	86	87	88	89	90
91	92	93	94	95	96	97	98	99	100

5 6 7 17
− 4 8
─────
1 9

5. Carrie hiked 0.75 mile before lunch and 0.40 mile after lunch. How much farther did she hike in the morning than in the afternoon?

$$\begin{array}{r} 75 \\ -40 \\ \hline 35 \end{array}$$

She hiked 0.35 more

1	2	3	4	5	6	7	8	9	10
11	12	13	14	15	16	17	18	19	20
21	22	23	24	25	26	27	28	29	30
31	32	33	34	35	36	37	38	39	40
41	42	43	44	45	46	47	48	49	50
51	52	53	54	55	56	57	58	59	60
61	62	63	64	65	66	67	68	69	70
71	72	73	74	75	76	77	78	79	80
81	82	83	84	85	86	87	88	89	90
91	92	93	94	95	96	97	98	99	100

6. Chad has a board that is 0.80 meter long. He trims 0.09 meter off the board. What is the length of the board now?

0.71

$$\begin{array}{r} 1\,8\,0\,10 \\ -6 \\ \hline 74 \end{array}$$

1	2	3	4	5	6	7	8	9	10
11	12	13	14	15	16	17	18	19	20
21	22	23	24	25	26	27	28	29	30
31	32	33	34	35	36	37	38	39	40
41	42	43	44	45	46	47	48	49	50
51	52	53	54	55	56	57	58	59	60
61	62	63	64	65	66	67	68	69	70
71	72	73	74	75	76	77	78	79	80
81	82	83	84	85	86	87	88	89	90
91	92	93	94	95	96	97	98	99	100

7. Derek left his house with $0.83 in his pocket. Some coins fell out of his pocket, and he has $0.57 now. How much money fell out of Derek's pocket?

$0.26

1	2	3	4	5	6	7	8	9	10
11	12	13	14	15	16	17	18	19	20
21	22	23	24	25	26	27	28	29	30
31	32	33	34	35	36	37	38	39	40
41	42	43	44	45	46	47	48	49	50
51	52	53	54	55	56	57	58	59	60
61	62	63	64	65	66	67	68	69	70
71	72	73	74	75	76	77	78	79	80
81	82	83	84	85	86	87	88	89	90
91	92	93	94	95	96	97	98	99	100

8. Eve gives a clerk $0.90 for a pen that costs $0.82, including tax. How much change does Eve receive?

0.03

$$\begin{array}{r} 8\,9\,0\,10 \\ -82 \\ \hline 03 \end{array}$$

1	2	3	4	5	6	7	8	9	10
11	12	13	14	15	16	17	18	19	20
21	22	23	24	25	26	27	28	29	30
31	32	33	34	35	36	37	38	39	40
41	42	43	44	45	46	47	48	49	50
51	52	53	54	55	56	57	58	59	60
61	62	63	64	65	66	67	68	69	70
71	72	73	74	75	76	77	78	79	80
81	82	83	84	85	86	87	88	89	90
91	92	93	94	95	96	97	98	99	100

Equivalent Fractions and Decimals

Fractions and decimals are ways of expressing a part of a whole. Fractions and decimals can be equivalent to each other. The word form is the key to figuring out the equivalence of decimals and fractions.

 **Example**

What decimal is equivalent to $\frac{5}{10}$?

The model shows 5 out of 10 shaded squares.

You can say that each square is a tenth. How many tenths are shaded?

Five of them are. So $\frac{5}{10}$ is the same as five-tenths, or 0.5.

Example

What fraction is equivalent to 0.25?

Say the word form of 0.25: twenty-five hundredths. The word form helps you find the fraction: Twenty-five is the numerator, and hundredths is the denominator.

$$0.25 = \frac{25}{100}$$

A model can help you find more than one equivalent decimal or fraction.

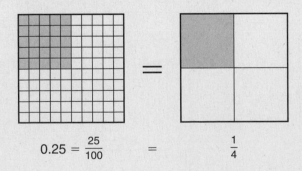

$$0.25 = \frac{25}{100} \qquad = \qquad \frac{1}{4}$$

The decimal 0.25 is equivalent to both $\frac{25}{100}$ and $\frac{1}{4}$.

You can also use a number line to find equivalent decimals and fractions.

Example

This number line shows tenths and fifths written as equivalent decimals and fractions.

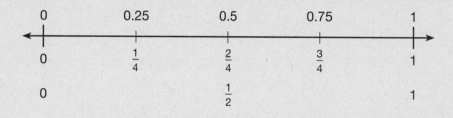

This number line shows fourths and halves written as equivalent decimals and fractions.

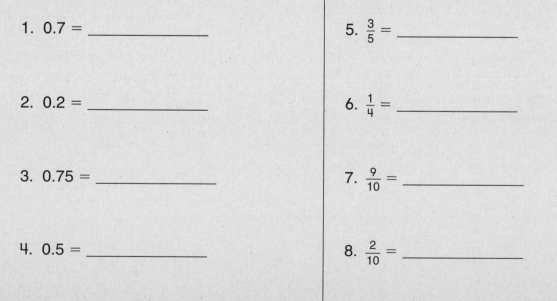

Practice

Directions: For questions 1 through 4, use the number lines above to write a fraction that is equivalent to the given decimal.

1. 0.7 = _____

2. 0.2 = _____

3. 0.75 = _____

4. 0.5 = _____

Directions: For questions 5 through 8, use the number lines above to write a decimal that is equivalent to the given fraction.

5. $\frac{3}{5}$ = _____

6. $\frac{1}{4}$ = _____

7. $\frac{9}{10}$ = _____

8. $\frac{2}{10}$ = _____

Directions: For questions 9 through 14, write a fraction and equivalent decimal to represent the shaded part of the figures.

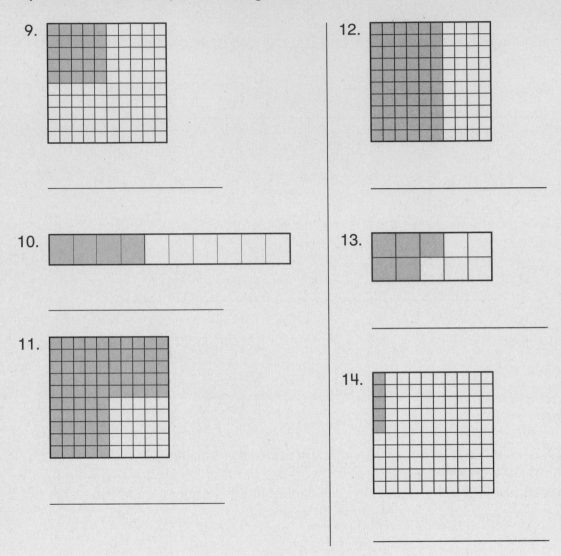

9.

_____

10.

_____

11.

_____

12.

_____

13.

_____

14.

_____

15. Last week, gym class was indoors 2 of the 5 school days because of rain. Shade the figure below to show what part of the 5 days of gym class was indoors. Then write a fraction and equivalent decimal that describe what part of last week's gym class was indoors.

_____

New York Math Practice begins on the following page.

New York Math Practice

1   Serena used the hundreds chart shown below to solve a subtraction problem.

1	2	3	4	5	6	7	8	9	10
11	12	13	14	15	16	17	18	19	20
21	22	23	24	25	26	27	28	29	30
31	32	33	34	35	36	37	38	39	40
41	42	43	44	45	46	47	48	⨂	⨂
⨂	⨂	⨂	⨂	⨂	⨂	⨂	⨂	⨂	⨂
⨂	⨂	⨂	⨂	⨂	66	67	68	69	70
71	72	73	74	75	76	77	78	79	80
81	82	83	84	85	86	87	88	89	90
91	92	93	94	95	96	97	98	99	100

What number sentence does the hundreds chart represent?

A $0.65 - 0.15 = 0.48$

B $0.65 - 0.17 = 0.48$

C $0.66 - 0.15 = 0.49$

D $0.66 - 0.17 = 0.48$

2   Kevin shaded 0.40 of this model.

Which fraction is equivalent to 0.40?

A $\frac{2}{5}$

B $\frac{4}{5}$

C $\frac{2}{10}$

D $\frac{6}{10}$

3 Lee drew this model of a decimal.

Which decimal does the shaded part of the model represent?

A 0.09

B 0.1

C 0.9

D 0.91

4 The coins Kayla uses to pay for a bracelet are shown below.

Which is the cost of the bracelet?

A $0.14

B $0.68

C $0.76

D $0.86

5 Which decimal is represented by the shaded part of this model?

A   0.40

B   0.49

C   0.50

D   0.59

6 Which decimal correctly completes this sentence?

0.47 > _____

A   0.49

B   0.47

C   0.05

D   0.50

7 Eric has a coin collection. Coins from the United States make up 0.3 of his collection. Coins from Asia make up 0.24 of his collection. Which number sentence correctly compares Eric's coins from the United States and Asia?

A $0.24 > 0.03$

B $0.24 > 0.3$

C $0.30 < 0.24$

D $0.3 > 0.24$

8 Tom has 2 quarters and 3 nickels in his pocket. Mae has 5 dimes and 7 pennies in her pocket. Leah has 1 quarter and 3 dimes in her pocket. Jamal has 2 quarters and 1 dime in his pocket. Who has the most money?

A   Tom

B   Mae

C   Leah

D   Jamal

9 Kiera has these coins.

Does Kiera have enough money to buy a marker that costs $0.79?

Answer _____

On the lines below, explain your thinking.

_____

_____

10   Pedro is riding his bike home from his friend's house. He rides 0.38 mile. Then his bike gets a flat tire. He has to walk his bike another $\frac{1}{4}$ mile to get home.

Part A

Shade the grid to represent the distance Pedro has to walk.

Part B

What decimal is equivalent to $\frac{1}{4}$?

Answer _____

Part C

How far does Pedro travel to get home? Use the hundreds chart to help you solve the problem.

1	2	3	4	5	6	7	8	9	10
11	12	13	14	15	16	17	18	19	20
21	22	23	24	25	26	27	28	29	30
31	32	33	34	35	36	37	38	39	40
41	42	43	44	45	46	47	48	49	50
51	52	53	54	55	56	57	58	59	60
61	62	63	64	65	66	67	68	69	70
71	72	73	74	75	76	77	78	79	80
81	82	83	84	85	86	87	88	89	90
91	92	93	94	95	96	97	98	99	100

Answer _____ mile

Lesson 5: Estimation and Problem Solving

Estimation tells you what number the answer to a problem should be close to. You can use estimation to make sure your answer is **reasonable** (makes sense).

Rounding Whole Numbers

Rounding is the most common way to estimate. To round any whole number or decimal:

- Circle the digit to be rounded to.
- Underline the number to the right of the circled digit.
- Decide whether the circled digit should stay the same or increase by 1.

  If the underlined number is **less than 5**, the circled digit **stays the same**.

  If the underlined number is **5 or greater**, the circled digit **increases by 1**.

- For a whole number, write a zero or zeros as placeholders after the rounded digit.

Example

Round 249 to the nearest hundred.

The 2 is in the hundreds place, so circle it. The 4 is to the right of the 2, so underline it.

②4̲ 9

Because 4 is less than 5, the 2 stays the same. Write zeros as placeholders to the right of the 2.

Therefore, 249 rounded to the nearest hundred is 200.

Example

Round 276 to the nearest ten.

The 7 is in the tens place, so circle it. The 6 is to the right of the 7, so underline it.

2 ⑦ 6

Because 6 is greater than 5, the 7 increases by 1 to 8. Write a zero after the rounded digit.

Therefore, 276 rounded to the nearest ten is 280.

Practice

1. Round 143 to the nearest: ten _____ hundred _____

2. Round 519 to the nearest: ten _____ hundred _____

3. Round 792 to the nearest: ten _____ hundred _____

4. Round 453 to the nearest: ten _____ hundred _____

5. Round 572 to the nearest: ten _____ hundred _____

6. Round 426 to the nearest: ten _____ hundred _____

7. What is 259 rounded to the nearest hundred?

    A. 200

    B. 260

    C. 300

    D. 350

8. What is 108 rounded to the nearest ten?

    A. 100

    B. 110

    C. 118

    D. 200

Rounding in Computation

You can use estimation when you compute. This will help you check your math to make sure your answer is reasonable. If the answer is not close to the estimated answer, go back and look for an error in the computation. You can also estimate when an exact answer is not necessary.

Round each of the numbers in the math problem. The place value you round to will depend on what numbers are in the problem.

Example

Estimate the sum of 345 and 487.

Round 345 to 300. Round 487 to 500.

Add the rounded amounts: 300 + 500 = 800.

Add the actual amounts: 345 + 487 = 832.

The estimated sum of 800 is close to the actual sum of 832.

Example

Estimate the product of 48 and 9.

Round 48 to 50. Do **not** round one-digit numbers, such as 9.

Multiply the rounded amount: 50 × 9 = 450.

Multiply the actual amounts: 48 × 9 = 432.

The estimated product of 450 is close to the actual product of 432.

Example

Estimate the difference of 51 and 28.

Round 51 to 50 and 28 to 30.

Subtract the rounded amounts: 50 − 30 = 20

Subtract the actual amounts: 51 − 28 = 23

The estimated difference of 20 is close to the actual difference of 23.

Practice

Directions: For questions 1 through 8, use rounding to find the estimated sum, difference, product, or quotient. Then find the actual answer.

1. 765 + 276

    estimate _____

    actual _____

2. 57 × 8

    estimate _____

    actual _____

3. 52 ÷ 9

    estimate _____

    actual _____

4. 82 − 36

    estimate _____

    actual _____

5. 29 × 7

    estimate _____

    actual _____

6. 879 − 299

    estimate _____

    actual _____

7. 416 ÷ 7

    estimate _____

    actual _____

8. 257 + 719

    estimate _____

    actual _____

Problem Solving

You can use a step-by-step strategy for solving problems whether you're inside or outside of the classroom. The practice activity will take you through this strategy.

Practice

Directions: Read the following information. Then, use the step-by-step strategy to help you solve the problem.

A cave tour charges $18 admission for adults and $12 admission for children. Pete's family is planning to take a cave tour with his cousin Tyler's family. Altogether there will be 4 adults and 7 children. How much will admission cost for Pete's family and Tyler's family together?

Step 1: **Understand the problem.**

1. What is the question that needs to be answered?

_____

2. What information is given in the problem?

_____

_____

_____

Step 2: **Decide what operation(s) you will need to solve the problem.**

3. Circle the operation(s) you will need to solve this problem.

addition   subtraction   multiplication   division

Step 3: **Set up the equation(s).**

4. number of adults × _____ = cost for adults

5. number of children × _____ = cost for children

6. cost for _____ + cost for _____ = total cost

Step 4: **Estimate.** (Round the cost of each admission price to the nearest ten dollars.)

      7. adult admission → _____

      8. child admission → _____

Use the rounded estimates in the equations from Step 3.

      9. _____ × _____ = _____

   10. _____ × _____ = _____

   11. _____ + _____ = _____

   12. The total estimated cost for Pete's family and Tyler's family is about

      _____.

Step 5: **Do the math with the actual values and check to make sure your answer is reasonable.**

   13. _____ × _____ = _____

   14. _____ × _____ = _____

   15. _____ + _____ = _____

   16. The total actual cost for Pete's family and Tyler's family is _____.

   17. Is your answer close to your estimate in Step 4? _____

Directions: For questions 18 through 23, show an estimate and the actual answer.

18. The students at an elementary school in Brookville volunteered to help clean up around the building. The first day, 45 students volunteered. The second day, 40 different students volunteered. How many students volunteered in all?

    Estimate: _____ students

    There were _____ students who volunteered.

19. Jamal had 295 sports trading cards. He gave 74 to his older brother and 28 to his younger brother. How many trading cards does Jamal have left?

    Estimate: _____ cards

    Jamal was left with _____ cards.

20. There were 171 students that signed up for the town basketball league. Each team will have 9 players. Every student that signs up will be on a team. How many teams will there be in the league?

    Estimate: _____ teams

    There will be _____ teams in the league.

21. Mr. Green teaches 8 different English classes. Each class has a total of 26 students. How many students does Mr. Green teach in all?

    Estimate: _____ students

    Mr. Green has _____ students.

22. Carmen spent $18 of her birthday money on a CD. She spent another $36 at the toy store. She had $13 left. How much money did Carmen receive for her birthday?

    Estimate: _____

    Carmen received _____ for her birthday.

23. There are 133 fourth-grade students at Lincoln Elementary School. For track-and-field day, they will run the 200-meter dash in groups of 7. How many groups of 7 will there be?

    Estimate: _____ groups

    There will be _____ groups.

Problem-Solving Strategies

For some problems, you may need to do more than write equations. Problem-solving strategies help you decide what to do. Here is a list of some strategies you can use to help you solve problems:

- Make a table (chart) or graph.
- Find a pattern.
- Use logical reasoning.
- Solve a simpler problem.
- Break the problem into parts.
- Work backward.

Make a Table (Chart) or Graph

Making a table or graph can help you organize information.

Example

Mr. Jennings's farm has 5 acres of corn and 9 acres of beans. Mrs. Crockett's farm has 3 acres of corn and 5 acres of beans. Mr. McDonald's farm has 7 acres of corn and 8 acres of beans. How many more acres of beans do the farms have than acres of corn?

There is a lot of information in this problem. Each sentence contains the same information but with different numbers.

A **table** will help you organize this information.

Farm	Acres of Corn	Acres of Beans
Mr. Jennings	5	9
Mrs. Crockett	3	5
Mr. McDonald	7	8
Total	15	22

Now that you have the information organized in a table, you can subtract the total number of acres of corn from the total number of acres of beans.

$$22 - 15 = 7$$

The farms have 7 more acres of beans than acres of corn.

Performance Indicator: 4.N.15

Find a Pattern

There are times when the given information follows a pattern that can be extended to solve the problem. Patterns will be covered in greater detail in Lesson 6.

Example

Maria is planting trees every week. Every week she plants three times as many trees as the week before. The 1st week she planted 1 tree, the 2nd week she planted 3 trees, the 3rd week she planted 9 trees, and so on. How many trees will Maria plant in the 6th week?

The number of trees Maria plants every week follows a number pattern. Each number is 3 times the previous number. Extend the number pattern to find how many trees Maria will plant in the 6th week.

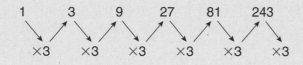

Maria will plant 243 trees in the 6th week.

Use Logical Reasoning

Logical reasoning involves carefully reading each part of the problem, and then seeing how the parts might fit together.

Example

Kristin, Lydia, Randy, and Justin are in a long jump competition. The boys did not finish the competition next to each other. The girls did not finish the competition next to each other. Justin finished last. Kristin finished ahead of Lydia. In what order did the four students finish in the competition?

You know that Justin finished last. Since neither the boys nor the girls finished next to each other, Randy must have finished second. Finally, since Kristin finished ahead of Lydia, Kristin must have finished first and Lydia must have finished third.

The order in which the four students finished the competition is Kristin, Randy, Lydia, and Justin.

Solve a Simpler Problem

Sometimes it helps to solve a problem that is similar to but simpler than your problem. You can then use the answer from the simpler problem to solve the more difficult problem.

Example

Juan has one red, one blue, one white, and one black pair of shorts. He also has one yellow, one orange, one white, one purple, and one green T-shirt. How many different combinations of one pair of shorts and one T-shirt does Juan have to choose from?

Instead of writing out all the different combinations, write out the combinations if Juan chooses the red pair of shorts.

red shorts, yellow T-shirt

red shorts, orange T-shirt

red shorts, white T-shirt

red shorts, purple T-shirt

red shorts, green T-shirt

There are 5 different combinations if Juan chooses the red pair of shorts.

There are 4 different pairs of shorts. Each pair of shorts will have 5 different combinations to choose from. So multiply:

$4 \times 5 = 20$

There are 20 different combinations that Juan can choose from.

Performance Indicator: 4.N.15

Break the Problem into Parts

You can break the problem into different parts, solve each part, and then put the solutions together for your final answer.

Example

At a concession stand, there were 45 small drinks sold for $2 each, 32 medium drinks sold for $3 each, and 74 large drinks sold for $4 each. What were the total sales of all drinks?

Break the problem into three parts. First find the total sales of small drinks.

$$45 \times 2 = 90$$

The total sales of small drinks were $90.

Then find the total sales of medium drinks.

$$32 \times 3 = 96$$

The total sales of medium drinks were $96.

Finally, find the total sales of large drinks.

$$74 \times 4 = 296$$

The total sales of large drinks were $296.

Now add the total sales of small, medium, and large drinks.

$$90 + 96 + 296 = 482$$

The total sales of all drinks were $482.

Work Backward

If you know a total amount, you can work backward to find a starting amount.

Example

Julie, Daniel, and Melissa were discussing the number of pages that each of them read over the weekend. Daniel read 10 more pages than Melissa. Julie read 2 times as many pages as Daniel. Julie read 84 pages. How many pages did Melissa read?

Work backward using the operations that are opposite to the given operations in the problem. Start with Julie and find how many pages Daniel read.

$$84 \div 2 = 42$$ **(Dividing by 2 is the opposite of "2 times.")**

Daniel read 42 pages.

Use the number of pages Daniel read to find how many pages Melissa read.

$$42 - 10 = 32$$ **(Subtracting 10 is the opposite of "10 more than.")**

Melissa read 32 pages.

Practice

Directions: For questions 1 through 7, choose a problem-solving strategy and solve each problem. Then tell which strategy you used and explain why you picked it to solve the problem.

1. April has 7 bags of beads containing 68 beads each. McKenzie has 4 bags of beads containing 33 beads each. How many beads do April and McKenzie have altogether?

   April and McKenzie have _____ beads altogether.

   _____

   _____

2. There are 6 teams in a soccer tournament. Each team plays each of the other teams once. How many total games will be played in the tournament?

There will be _____ total games played in the tournament.

_____

_____

3. Kirk won a bag of candy at the county fair. He gave 14 pieces of candy to Sean, 7 pieces of candy to Stephany, 12 pieces of candy to Allison, and kept 17 pieces of candy for himself. How many pieces of candy were in the bag to start with?

The bag started with _____ pieces of candy.

_____

_____

4. Ethan was given this letter pattern: A D G J M P __ __. He was asked to fill in the blanks. What letters should Ethan use to fill in the blanks?

Ethan should use the letters _____ and _____ to fill in the blanks.

_____

_____

5. Four friends kept track of the number of books they each read last year. Sallie read 2 times as many books as Rachel. Todd read 5 more books than Rachel. Collin read 11 fewer books than Todd. Sallie read a total of 28 books last year. How many books did Collin read?

    Collin read _____ books last year.

    _____

    _____

6. Jerry is renting a kayak for a 5-day vacation in the Allegheny National Forest. It costs $55 to rent the kayak for the first day and $45 for each additional day. How much will Jerry spend to rent the kayak for 5 days?

    Jerry will spend _____ to rent the kayak for 5 days.

    _____

    _____

7. The top three finishers in a swimming race each finished within 0.05 seconds of each other. The winning time was 23.04 seconds. Leslie finished after Karin. Meredith had a time of 23.09 seconds. Who won the race?

    _____ won the race.

    _____

    _____

New York Math Practice

1 Yoshi has 346 insects in his collection. To the nearest ten, about how many insects are in Yoshi's collection?

   A 300

   B 340

   C 350

   D 400

2 Which number rounded to the nearest hundred is 200?

   A 118

   B 152

   C 257

   D 263

3 The table below shows the number of students who went to the movies.

MOVIES

Day	Number of Students
Thursday	54
Friday	62
Saturday	45

Which is the **best** estimate for the total number of students who went to the movies?

   A 150

   B 160

   C 170

   D 180

4   Four students are standing in line. Ann is behind Maria and in front of Jose. Maria is behind Carl. In what order are the students standing?

   A   Carl, Maria, Ann, Jose

   B   Maria, Ann, Jose, Carl

   C   Ann, Jose, Carl, Maria

   D   Jose, Carl, Maria, Ann

5   A coach spent $40 on 9 soccer balls. He estimated that each soccer ball cost about $4. Is his estimate reasonable?

   A   It is reasonable because $36 \div 9 = 4$.

   B   It is reasonable because $32 \div 8 = 4$.

   C   It is not reasonable because $40 \div 8 = 5$.

   D   It is not reasonable because $42 \div 7 = 6$.

6   Mr. Berry has 3 boxes of markers. Each box contains 12 markers. Which expression could be used to find the total number of markers?

   A $3 + 12$

   B $12 + 12$

   C 3×12

   D 12×12

7   Mrs. Guille had 529 stickers. She used 407 stickers. Which expression can be used to **estimate** the number of stickers Mrs. Guille has left?

   A $500 + 400 = 900$

   B $500 - 400 = 100$

   C $550 - 410 = 140$

   D $600 - 400 = 200$

8 Tina's grandparents gave her some money to spend at the arts and craft store. She spent $7 for a sketch pad and $9 for a box of colored pencils. She has $8 left. How much money did Tina's grandparents give her?

A $8

B $16

C $17

D $24

9 Evan is helping Carrie move. Evan moved 3 stacks of 7 boxes. Carrie moved 6 stacks of 4 boxes. There are 60 boxes in all. How many boxes are left to move?

A 45

B 24

C 21

D 15

10 Ms. Thomas had 529 stickers. She used 392. Estimate the number of stickers Ms. Thomas has left. Then find the actual answer.

Show your work.

Estimate: _____ stickers

Answer: _____ stickers

11 Heather has 36 trading cards. She wants to keep 6 of them and divide the rest equally among 3 friends. How many cards will each friend get?

Part A

What operations are needed to solve this problem?

Answer: _____

Part B

How many total cards will Heather give away?

Show your work.

Answer: _____ cards

Part C

How many cards will each friend get?

Show your work.

Answer: _____ cards

Unit 2

Algebra

Patterns are almost everywhere you look. Think about the tiles that make up your kitchen floor or the polka dots on your favorite shirt. You can usually describe a pattern by using a rule to get to the next shape or number.

Algebra is all about solving problems when there is something missing. What's missing is usually a number. Your job is to find the number that will solve the problem.

In this unit, you will find the missing shape or number in a pattern and write the rule for the pattern. You will also use symbols to represent missing numbers and determine the values of these missing numbers.

In This Unit

Patterns

Algebra

Lesson 6: Patterns

There are many kinds of patterns throughout the world. In this lesson, you will identify, describe, and extend geometric and numeric patterns.

Geometric Patterns

Geometric patterns are made up of shapes. A geometric pattern usually repeats the shapes that make up the pattern.

Example

Look at the pattern of the shapes and describe the geometric pattern.

There is one big star followed by a planet, a little star, and a quarter moon. After the quarter moon is another big star. This shows that the pattern is repeating.

These four guidelines will help you find what figure comes next in a geometric pattern.

- **Look at the shapes of the figures.**

Pattern: triangle, square, star, triangle, square, star.

The next figure in the pattern is a **triangle**.

- **Look at the sizes of the figures.**

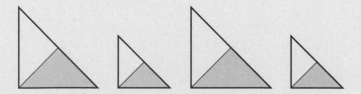

Pattern: big triangle, small triangle, big triangle, small triangle.

The next figure in the pattern is a **big triangle**.

- **Look at the shading or marks in the figures.**

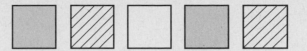

This pattern has the same shape, but the squares are colored differently: shaded, striped, blank, shaded, striped.

The next figure in the pattern is a **blank square**.

- **Look at the number and arrangement of items in each figure of the pattern.**

★ ★ ★ ★ ★ ★ ★ ★ ★ ★ ★ ★ ★ ★ ★
★ ★ ★ ★ ★ ★ ★ ★ ★ ★ ★ ★ ★ ★ ★
★ ★ ★ ★ ★ ★ ★ ★ ★ ★ ★ ★ ★ ★ ★

This pattern has three stars in each column. Each figure of this pattern has one more column of stars than the figure before it.

The next figure of this pattern will have **6 columns with 3 stars in each column.**

TIP: You may need more than one of these guidelines to find the next figure in a geometric pattern.

Practice

1. Create your own geometric pattern using circles ◯ and triangles △.

2. Describe your geometric pattern.

_____

_____

_____

Directions: For questions 3 through 5, draw the next three figures for each pattern. Then, describe the pattern.

3.

_____ _____ _____

Describe the pattern. _____

_____

_____

4.

_____ _____ _____

Describe the pattern. _____

_____

_____

5.

_____ _____ _____

Describe the pattern. _____

_____

_____

Performance Indicator: 4.A.4

Numeric Patterns

There are many kinds of **numeric patterns**. As with geometric patterns, you need to figure out the rule for a pattern to find a missing number or the next number. All four mathematical operations ($+$, $-$, $\times$, $\div$) can be used to make a pattern. A rule can be written using symbols or words as shown below.

Example

What is the rule for the pattern? What is the missing number?

3; 12; _____; 192; 768; 3,072

The numbers in this pattern are increasing rapidly. That means it's probably a multiplication pattern. The rule is **multiply by 4 ($\times$4)**. The missing number in the pattern is **48**.

Example

What is the rule for the pattern? What is the next number?

1, 7, 4, 10, 7, 13, 10, 16, 13, . . .

In this pattern, the numbers increase by 6, then decrease by 3. The rule is **add 6, subtract 3 ($+$6, $-$3)**. The next number is 19.

Practice

Directions: For questions 1 through 5, fill in the missing numbers and write the rule for each pattern using symbols and numbers.

1. 5; 15; 45; _____; 405, _____; 3,645   The rule is _____.

2. 55, 53, 51, _____, 47, 45, 43, _____   The rule is _____.

3. 4; 5; 50; _____; 510; 511; 5,110; 5,111   The rule is _____.

4. 9,216; 2,304; _____; _____; 36; 9   The rule is _____.

5. _____; 20; _____; 2,000; 20,000   The rule is _____.

Directions: For questions 6 and 7, use the numeric pattern to answer the questions.

6. 5, 14, 10, 19, 15, 24, . . .

   What is the rule for the pattern? _____

   What is the eighth number in this pattern? _____

7. 2,187; 729; 243; 81; . . .

   What is the rule for the pattern? _____

   What is the sixth number in this pattern? _____

8. Write six terms of a pattern that follows the rule ×2, −1.

   _____

9. Write your own numeric pattern and explain the rule you used.

   _____

   _____

   _____

10. Every Monday, Trina writes in a notebook the number of days left before her birthday. So far, she has written these numbers: 50, 43, 36, 29. Next Monday, how many days will be left before Trina's birthday?

    _____

11. Clark was riding his bicycle down the sidewalk. He was looking at the addresses on each house as he went by. The first four addresses he saw were 2455, 2485, 2515, and 2545. What address do you think Clark will see next? Explain your answer.

    _____

    _____

Performance Indicator: 4.A.5

Input/Output Tables

An **input/output table** (also called a **function table**) matches each input value to its output value. You can find the rule for an input/output table by looking for the pattern between the input and output values. Sometimes, *x* and *y* are used as headings in the table instead of input and output.

Example

What is the rule for going from the input column to the output column?

Input	Output
1	6
3	8
5	10
7	12

Each number in the output column is 5 more than the number in the input column. The rule for going from the input column to the output column is **+5**.

Example

What is the rule for going from column *x* to column *y*? What is the missing value?

x	*y*
2	6
4	12
6	
8	24

The rule for going from column *x* to column *y* is **multiply by 3**.

Multiply 6 by 3 to find the missing value in the function table.

$6 \times 3 = 18$

The missing value in the function table is **18**.

Practice

Directions: For questions 1 through 3, find the rule.

Directions: For questions 4 through 6, find the missing value in the table.

1.
Input	Output
20	11
18	9
15	6
11	2

4.
Input	Output
1	7
4	28
7	49
11	

2.
Input	Output
2	31
5	34
6	35
9	38

5.
Input	Output
3	15
4	16
7	19
9	

3.
x	y
11	9
7	5
4	2
2	0

6.
x	y
99	49
87	37
74	
68	18

Directions: Use the information and table to answer questions 7 and 8.

Tasha planted the same number of flowers each week for seven weeks. She made the table to show the total number of flowers she had planted after each week.

Week	1	2	3	4	5	6	7
Total Number of Flowers	8	16	24				

7. What is the rule for going from the first row to the second row in the table?

8. Fill in the missing numbers in the table.

New York Math Practice begins on the following page.

New York Math Practice

1   Lynn drew the geometric pattern shown below.

Which rule **best** describes her pattern?

A   big square, small square, big square, small square

B   big shaded square, small shaded square, big shaded square, small shaded square

C   big square, small shaded square, big square, small shaded square

D   big shaded square, small square, big shaded square, small square

2   Natalie made this table.

Input	Output
4	9
6	11
8	13
10	15

Which rule could be used to find each Output number?

A   Add 4 to the Input number.

B   Add 5 to the Input number.

C   Multiply the Input number by 2.

D   Multiply the Input number by 3.

3 Hannah draws the pattern below.

What figure should she draw next?

A ☐

B ◯

C △

D ⬭

4 Renee wrote a pattern that follows the rule −9. Which of the following patterns could she have written?

A 5, 6, 7, 8, 9

B 1, 10, 19, 28, 37

C 9, 8, 7, 6, 5

D 47, 38, 29, 20, 11

5 Malik writes this pattern.

5, 8, 11, _____, 17, 20

Which is the missing number in Malik's pattern?

A 12

B 13

C 14

D 16

6 Lemont made the table shown below.

Input	Output
3	9
12	36
15	45
21	63

What rule did Lemont use?

A   Add 6 to the Input number.

B   Add 9 to the Input number.

C   Multiply the Input number by 3.

D   Multiply the Input number by 12.

7 This table shows the relationship between feet and inches.

Feet	1	2	3	4	5	6
Inches	12	24	36	48		72

What number is missing from the table?

Show your work.

Answer: _____

8 Molly wrote the number pattern shown below.

3, 6, 12, 24

Part A

What are the next two numbers in Molly's pattern?

Answer: _____

Part B

What is the rule for Molly's pattern?

Rule: _____

Part C

Another pattern follows the same rule as Molly's pattern. The pattern begins with 5. What are the first three numbers of the new pattern?

Answer: _____

Performance Indicator: 4.A.1

Lesson 7: Algebra

Algebra uses expressions, number sentences, and inequalities to represent numbers and mathematical relationships.

Expressions

An **expression** is a number by itself or a number written using an operation sign such as $+$, $-$, $\times$, or $\div$. An expression does **not** have an equal sign ($=$) or an inequality sign ($<$ or $>$).

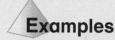

Examples

"Eight multiplied by nine" can be expressed as 8×9.

"Five fewer than seven" can be expressed as $7 - 5$.

Practice

Directions: For questions 1 through 5, write an expression to show the relationship given.

1. thirty-two plus five _____

2. nine times twenty-seven _____

3. four more than fifteen _____

4. seven less than sixty-four _____

5. four divided by two _____

6. Paige used 2 cups of flour to make 27 cookies. She took the cookies to school and gave one to each of her 22 classmates. Write an expression that could help you find how many cookies Paige has left.

_____

Writing Expressions

Expressions sometimes have missing numbers. Symbols, such as □, ○, △, and ▽, represent the missing numbers. You can also use letters called **variables** to represent missing numbers in an expression.

Examples

"A number plus twelve" can be expressed as □ + 12.

"Twenty-four divided by a number" can be expressed as 24 ÷ n.

Example

Cory biked 7 miles on the Northern Trail before he stopped for lunch. After lunch, he biked a few more miles on the trail. Write an expression that shows the total number of miles Cory biked altogether.

miles biked before lunch → 7 + ○ **← miles biked after lunch**

Practice

Directions: For questions 1 through 7, write an expression to show the relationship given. Use symbols or letters to represent missing numbers.

1. sixteen minus a number _____

2. a number multiplied by three _____

3. a number plus twenty-two _____

4. fifty-six divided by a number _____

5. the total of fifteen and a number _____

6. ten times a number _____

7. twenty-seven less than a number _____

Directions: For questions 8 through 12, write an expression to show the relationship given.

8. Jonathan read 6 books last month. Each book had the same number of pages.

   • Let *p* represent the number of pages in each book.

   Write an expression to show how many total pages Jonathan read.

   _____

9. Haley is 7 years older than her brother, Mike.

   • Let △ represent Mike's age.

   Write an expression showing how old Haley is.

   _____

10. Jana brought brownies to school. She gave one to each of the 24 students in her class.

    • Let *b* represent the number of brownies Jana brought to school.

    Write an expression to show how many brownies Jana has left.

    _____

11. Frank earned $22 working on Monday. He earned more money working on Tuesday.

    • Let *t* represent the amount Frank earned on Tuesday.

    Write an expression that shows how much money Frank earned on Monday and Tuesday.

    _____

12. Mrs. Rose put the same number of books on 8 shelves.

    • Let □ represent the number of books Mrs. Rose put on each shelf.

    Write an expression to find the total number of books Mrs. Rose put on the shelves.

    _____

Number Sentences

A **number sentence** shows two expressions that are related to each other. When the two expressions are equal to each other, this relationship is shown with an "equal to" symbol (=). When the two expression are not equal to each other, the "not equal to" symbol (≠) is used to show the relationship.

Example

Use = or ≠ to show how the expressions are related.

$84 \div 4$ ___ 3×7

Dividing 84 by 4 equals 21. Multiplying 3 and 7 equals 21. Therefore, the two expressions have the same value and are equal to each other.

$84 \div 4 = 3 \times 7$

Example

Use = or ≠ to complete the number sentence.

6×4 ___ $28 - 6$

Multiplying 6 and 4 equals 24. Subtracting 6 from 28 equals 22. Therefore the two expressions do not have the same value and are not equal to each other.

$6 \times 4 \neq 28 - 6$

Practice

Directions: For questions 1 through 8, use = or ≠ to complete the number sentences.

1. $19 + 36$ _____ $81 - 28$

2. $72 \div 4$ _____ $108 \div 6$

3. 17×3 _____ 25×2

4. 12×14 _____ 13×13

5. 6×5 _____ $8 + 22$

6. $64 - 7$ _____ 7×8

7. $54 \div 3$ _____ 6×3

8. $81 + 12$ _____ $190 \div 2$

Performance Indicator: 4.A.1

Open Number Sentences

Sometimes you will see a number sentence that has one or more numbers missing from it. Your job is to find the missing number or numbers.

Example

What number replaces the □ in this number sentence?

$6 + □ = 13$

You need to find out what number added to 6 will equal 13.

$6 + \mathbf{7} = 13$

The number **7** replaces the □ in the equation.

Example

What number replaces the □ in this number sentence?

$2 \times □ = 16$

You need to find out what number multiplied by 2 will equal 16.

$2 \times \mathbf{8} = 16$

The number **8** replaces the □ in the equation.

Example

What number replaces *n* in this number sentence?

$n - 2 = 7$

You need to find out what number you can subtract 2 from to equal 7.

$\mathbf{9} - 2 = 7$

The number **9** replaces *n* in the equation.

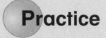

Practice

Directions: For questions 1 through 7, find the number that replaces each symbol.

1. $5 + \square = 8$ $\square =$ _____

2. $\bigcirc - 5 = 11$ $\bigcirc =$ _____

3. $\triangledown \times 6 = 24$ $\triangledown =$ _____

4. $14 - \square = 9$ $\square =$ _____

5. $\bigcirc + 3 = 12$ $\bigcirc =$ _____

6. $8 \times \triangledown = 56$ $\triangledown =$ _____

7. $20 \div \triangle = 5$ $\triangle =$ _____

8. What number replaces the $\square$ in this equation?

    $13 + \square = 22$

    A. 9
    B. 11
    C. 13
    D. 22

Directions: For questions 9 through 15, find the number that replaces each variable.

9. $n + 9 = 18$ $n =$ _____

10. $25 - c = 13$ $c =$ _____

11. $m \times 3 = 21$ $m =$ _____

12. $26 \div g = 13$ $g =$ _____

13. $6 + x = 15$ $x =$ _____

14. $p \times 7 = 35$ $p =$ _____

15. $48 \div h = 4$ $h =$ _____

16. What number replaces z in this equation?

    $32 \div z = 4$

    A. 4
    B. 6
    C. 8
    D. 9

Performance Indicator: 4.A.1

Writing Open Number Sentences

Sometimes you will be given a problem and you will have to write an open number sentence in order to solve the problem.

◢ Example

Tyra had $12 in her wallet yesterday. Today she received her weekly allowance. Now she has $15 in her wallet. What is Tyra's weekly allowance?

Use this addition open number sentence to solve the problem: $12 + n = 15$

amount in wallet yesterday → $12 + n = 15$ ← **amount in wallet today**

Tyra's weekly allowance amount (the missing number)

What number replaces n in the open number sentence?

$12 + n = 15$

$12 + \mathbf{3} = 15$

Tyra's weekly allowance is $3.

◢ Example

The owners of a tree farm planted 24 pine trees. They planted 6 trees in each row. How many rows did they plant?

Use this division open number sentence to solve the problem: $24 \div \square = 6$

total number of trees → $24 \div \square = 6$ ← **number of trees in each row**

number of rows (the missing number)

What number replaces the $\square$ in the open number sentence?

$24 \div \square = 6$

$24 \div \mathbf{4} = 6$

The owners planted 4 rows of pine trees.

Practice

Directions: For questions 1 through 5, write an open number sentence that can be used to solve each problem. Choose your own variable to represent the missing number. Then solve for the variable and give the answer.

1. Jasmine bought a gift for her brother. She paid for it with a $10 bill. The cashier gave her $3 back. How much did the gift cost?

   _____

2. Geoff read 3 books this summer. He read a total of 513 pages. If each book had the same number of pages, how many pages are in each book?

   _____

3. Lisa flipped a two-sided coin 17 times. The coin landed with heads facing up 11 times. How many times did the coin land with tails facing up?

   _____

4. Tim's mom bought some packages of hot dog buns for a barbecue. Each package contains 8 buns. She bought a total of 40 buns. How many packages of buns did Tim's mom buy?

   _____

5. Sydney and Adrianna took a math test. Sydney got 15 more points than Adrianna. If Sydney got 93 points, how many points did Adrianna get?

   _____

Performance Indicator: 4.A.1

Inequalities

An **inequality** is a number sentence that uses the symbols < (less than) or > (greater than).

Example

Write an inequality to show "34 more than a number is greater than 61."

The phrase "more than" means addition.

The phrase "is greater than" is shown by the symbol >.

The inequality is $34 + n > 61$.

Practice

Directions: For questions 1 through 7, write an inequality for each sentence.

1. A number divided by 5 is less than 25. _____

2. 8 times a number is greater than 80. _____

3. A number minus 164 is greater than 198. _____

4. 18 plus a number is less than 62. _____

5. 16 divided by a number is greater than 48. _____

6. A number plus 86 is less than 95. _____

7. A number minus 156 is greater than 197. _____

Solving Inequalities

You can solve an inequality to find the value of the missing numbers.

Example

What numbers replace the $\square$ in this inequality?

$16 + \square > 25$

You can solve the inequality by subtracting 16 from both sides because addition and subtraction are opposite operations.

$$16 + \square > 25$$
$$16 - \mathbf{16} + \square > 25 - \mathbf{16}$$
$$\square > 9$$

The numbers greater than 9 replace the $\square$ in the inequality.

Example

What numbers replace the $\bigcirc$ in this inequality?

$\bigcirc \times 3 < 24$

You can solve the inequality by dividing both sides by 3 because multiplication and division are opposite operations.

$$\bigcirc \times 3 < 24$$
$$\bigcirc \times 3 \div \mathbf{3} < 24 \div \mathbf{3}$$
$$\bigcirc < 8$$

The numbers less than 8 replace the $\bigcirc$ in the inequality.

Example

What numbers replace *n* in this inequality?

$n - 200 > 350$

You can solve the inequality by adding 200 to both sides because addition and subtraction are opposite operations.

$$n - 200 > 350$$
$$n - 200 + \mathbf{200} > 350 + \mathbf{200}$$
$$n > 550$$

The numbers greater than 550 replace *n* in this inequality.

Practice

Directions: For questions 1 through 24, find the numbers that can replace each symbol or variable to solve the inequality.

1. $\square \div 9 > 15$ $\square >$ _____
13. $z \div 5 < 25$ $z <$ _____

2. $\triangledown - 11 < 19$ $\triangledown <$ _____
14. $7 \times \bigcirc > 98$ $\bigcirc >$ _____

3. $54 + \bigcirc < 91$ $\bigcirc <$ _____
15. $77 + \square < 134$ $\square <$ _____

4. $3 \times \square > 27$ $\square >$ _____
16. $\triangledown - 38 < 46$ $\triangledown <$ _____

5. $\bigcirc \div 6 < 7$ $\bigcirc <$ _____
17. $\triangle \times 4 < 88$ $\triangle <$ _____

6. $\triangle + 45 > 93$ $\triangle >$ _____
18. $\bigcirc - 50 > 32$ $\bigcirc >$ _____

7. $n - 21 < 234$ $n <$ _____
19. $a \div 32 > 11$ $a >$ _____

8. $m \times 6 > 48$ $m >$ _____
20. $x - 106 < 15$ $x <$ _____

9. $59 + g < 94$ $g <$ _____
21. $p \div 20 < 25$ $p <$ _____

10. $t \times 7 < 56$ $t <$ _____
22. $30 \times n < 900$ $n <$ _____

11. $s \div 12 > 15$ $s >$ _____
23. $m - 14 > 256$ $m >$ _____

12. $e + 27 > 159$ $e >$ _____
24. $w \div 20 < 38$ $w <$ _____

New York Math Practice

1 Which numbers can replace y in the inequality below?

$6 \times y < 72$

A $y < 12$

B $y < 66$

C $y < 78$

D $y < 432$

2 Emily scored b baskets in her basketball game. Each basket was worth 2 points. Which expression shows how many points Emily scored?

A $b + 2$

B $b - 2$

C $b \times 2$

D $b \div 2$

3 Which symbol belongs on the line to make the number sentence correct?

$7 \times 8 \underline{\hspace{1cm}} 47 + 13$

A $=$

B $\neq$

C $>$

D $\times$

4 Which number replaces *s* in the number sentence below?

$s \div 3 = 13$

A   1

B   13

C   16

D   39

5 Katherine has a piggy bank that holds a total of 500 quarters. She has 273 quarters in her bank. She wrote this number sentence to help her find out how many more quarters she needs to fill her bank.

$273 + x = 500$

What does the variable *x* represent in the number sentence?

A   the total number of quarters

B   the number of quarters Katherine has in the bank

C   the number of quarters Katherine can add to the bank

D   the number of quarters Katherine took out of the bank

6 Which number could replace *n* in the inequality below?

$n - 19 > 12$

A   7

B   20

C   31

D   40

7 Chelsea bought a poster at the art museum for $15. She also bought a book. Together, the poster and book cost more than $25. Let b = the cost of the book. Which inequality could you solve to find how much Chelsea paid for the book?

A $15 + b > 25$

B $15 + b < 25$

C $b - 15 > 25$

D $15 \times b > 25$

8 There are 7 tables in one room of a restaurant. Each table has the same number of chairs. There are a total of 28 chairs. How many chairs are at each table?

Write a number sentence to find the number of chairs at each table. Then solve it.

Show your work.

Answer: _____ chairs

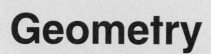

Unit 3

Geometry

Have you ever seen those structures made up of six-sided cells that bees create to store honey? They are called *honeycombs*. Surely you've seen an eight-sided stop sign. Whether you live in a large city or in the country, you are surrounded by many examples of geometry. You can find geometry in the construction of highway systems or in the markings of a butterfly. All you need to do is look.

In this unit, you will learn about geometric figures that are all around you. You will learn how to classify polygons and three-dimensional shapes. You will also learn how to find the perimeter of polygons and the area of rectangles.

In This Unit

Geometric Figures

Perimeter and Area

Lesson 8: Geometric Figures

When you study shapes, you are studying geometric figures. Here is a look at some basic vocabulary.

side: a line with two endpoints that makes up part of the outside of a figure

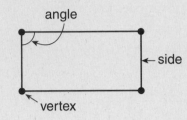

vertex: the point where two or more sides of a figure meet

angle: the space formed by two sides with a common vertex

Polygons

Polygons are closed plane figures made up of 3 or more straight sides. Polygons are named by the number of sides, angles, and vertices they have.

Triangle	Quadrilateral	Pentagon	Hexagon	Octagon
a polygon with 3 sides and 3 angles	a polygon with 4 sides and 4 angles	a polygon with 5 sides and 5 angles	a polygon with 6 sides and 6 angles	a polygon with 8 sides and 8 angles

Polygons that have 4 sides and 4 angles are **quadrilaterals**. These are some examples of quadrilaterals.

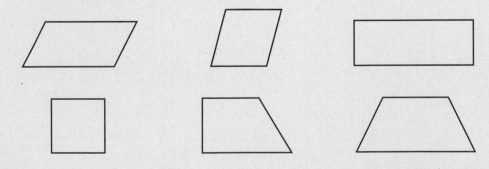

TIP: Regular polygons have the same measure for all their sides and angles. **Irregular polygons** do not have the same measures for all their sides and angles.

ractice

1. Under each real-world object, write the name of the polygon that it looks like.

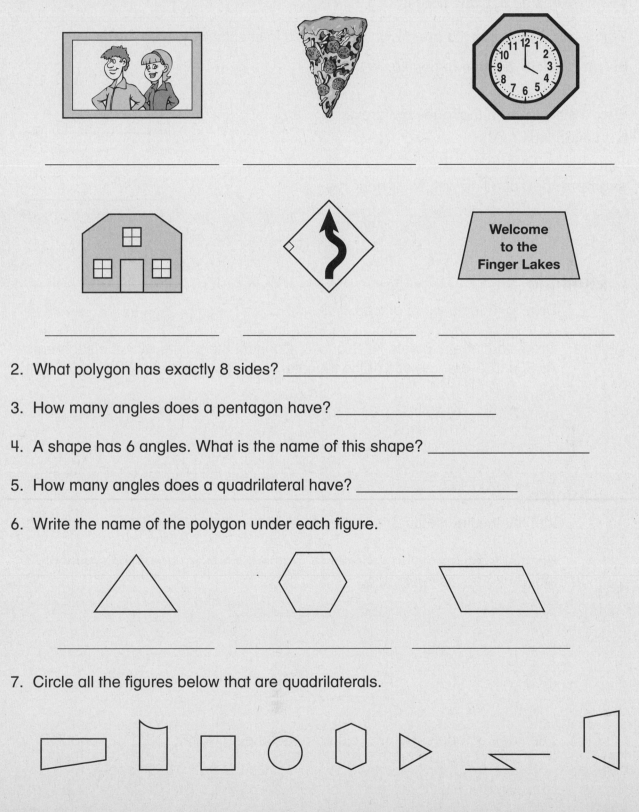

2. What polygon has exactly 8 sides? _____

3. How many angles does a pentagon have? _____

4. A shape has 6 angles. What is the name of this shape? _____

5. How many angles does a quadrilateral have? _____

6. Write the name of the polygon under each figure.

7. Circle all the figures below that are quadrilaterals.

139

Drawing Polygons

Plane figures are two-dimensional. That means they lie on a flat surface, having only a length and a width. Triangles, squares, rectangles, hexagons, and octagons are some examples of plane figures.

Points and line segments are drawn and labeled in special ways.

point: a single location or position (*R*)

line: a straight path that goes on forever in both directions ($\overleftrightarrow{AB}$)

segment: part of a line with two endpoints ($\overline{AB}$)

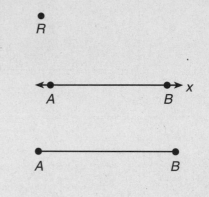

Example

Draw a triangle with vertices *A*, *B*, and *C*.

Draw and label 3 points *A*, *B*, and *C*. Connect the points with line segments. *A*, *B*, and *C* are vertices of the triangle.

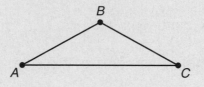

Example

Identify the line segments that make up the rectangle below.

Each side of the rectangle is a line segment, so there are 4 line segments that make up the rectangle.

The line segments that make up the rectangle are $\overline{WX}$, $\overline{XY}$, $\overline{YZ}$, and $\overline{ZW}$.

Performance Indicator: 4.G.2

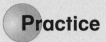 **Practice**

1. Draw a triangle with vertices *P*, *B*, and *J*.

What are the names of the line segments that make up the triangle?

_____

2. Draw a pentagon and label the vertices.

What are the names of the line segments that make up the pentagon?

_____

3. A hexagon has sides $\overline{AB}$, $\overline{BC}$, $\overline{CD}$, $\overline{DE}$, $\overline{EF}$, and $\overline{FA}$. Draw the hexagon and label the vertices.

Three-Dimensional Shapes

Three-dimensional shapes are solid figures with three dimensions: length, width, and height. The table below shows some different types of three-dimensional shapes.

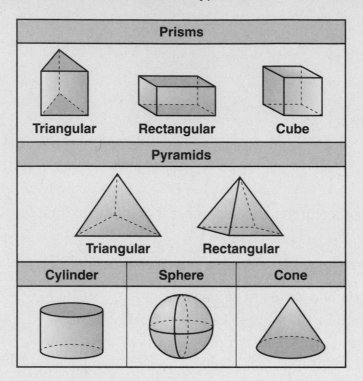

Practice

1. What three-dimensional shapes have curved surfaces?

_____

2. What three-dimensional shape has no flat surfaces? _____

3. What three-dimensional shape has exactly two flat surfaces? _____

4. What three-dimensional shape has exactly one flat surface? _____

5. Under each real-world object, write the name of the three-dimensional figure that it looks like.

6. Write down three objects in your classroom. Then write the name of the three-dimensional shape that each object looks like.

_____

_____

_____

7. How are a triangular pyramid and a cone the same?

_____

_____

8. How are a triangular pyramid and a cone different?

_____

_____

Faces, Edges, and Vertices

Some three-dimensional shapes have faces, edges, and vertices. The **faces** of three-dimensional shapes are plane figures. The segments formed where these faces meet are **edges**. Any point where edges meet is a **vertex**.

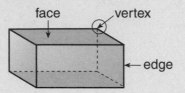

Practice

Directions: For questions 1 and 2, write a description of the object shown. Include the name of the three-dimensional shape, the shapes of the faces, and the number of faces, edges, and vertices.

1.
   _____
   _____
   _____

2.
   _____
   _____
   _____

3. Which plane figure below can be found on a cylinder?

   A. triangle

   B. square

   C. rectangle

   D. circle

4. Which polygon below makes up the base of a triangular pyramid?

   A. triangle

   B. rectangle

   C. circle

   D. square

New York Math Practice

1 Which of these three-dimensional shapes has 8 edges?

A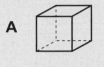

B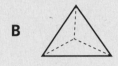

C

D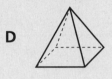

2 Jill drew a polygon with 5 sides. Which polygon did she draw?

   A hexagon

   B octagon

   C pentagon

   D quadrilateral

3 Darryl drew and labeled the rectangle shown below.

Which is a line segment in the rectangle?

A $\overline{GD}$

B $\overline{FD}$

C $\overline{DF}$

D $\overline{GE}$

4 Which polygon is a quadrilateral?

A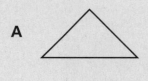

B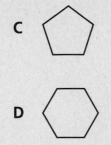

C

D

5 Which three-dimensional shape has two faces that are triangles and three faces that are rectangles?

    A   triangular prism

    B   triangular pyramid

    C   rectangular prism

    D   rectangular pyramid

6 How many angles does an octagon have?

    A   4

    B   5

    C   6

    D   8

7 Draw triangle EFG and label the vertices.

Name the line segments that make up your triangle.

*Answer*_____

Lesson 9: Perimeter and Area

Perimeter and area are two different ways to measure figures.

Perimeter

Perimeter (*P*) is the distance around the outside of a figure. To find the perimeter of a figure, add the lengths of all its sides.

Example

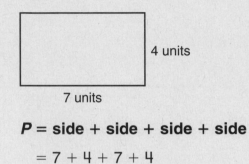

What is the perimeter of this rectangle?

4 units

7 units

$$P = \text{side} + \text{side} + \text{side} + \text{side}$$

$$= 7 + 4 + 7 + 4$$

$$= 22$$

The perimeter of the rectangle is 22 units.

Practice

Directions: For questions 1 through 5, find the perimeter of each figure.

1.

8 cm

17 cm

$P = $ _____

2.

19 ft

19 ft

$P = $ _____

3.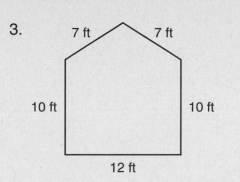

P = _____

4.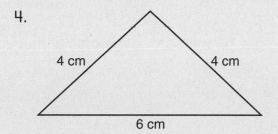

P = _____

5.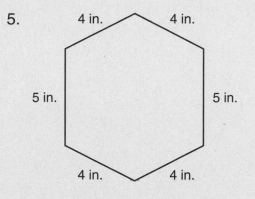

P = _____

6. Max is helping his dad put a fence around their rectangular garden patch. The longer side of the patch measures 21 feet. The shorter side measures 8 feet. What is the perimeter of the garden?

P = _____

7. Sallie is putting a border around a quilt. The longer side of the quilt measures 11 feet. The shorter side measures 8 feet. What is the perimeter of the quilt?

P = _____

Area

Area (A) is the number of **square units** that cover a figure. To find the area of a rectangle, count the number of squares needed to cover the rectangle.

Example

What is the area of this rectangle?

Count the total number of squares. There are 18 squares, so the area of the rectangle is 18 square units.

Practice

Directions: For questions 1 through 5, find the area of each figure.

1.

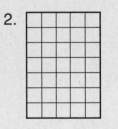

A = _____

2.

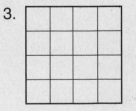

A = _____

3.

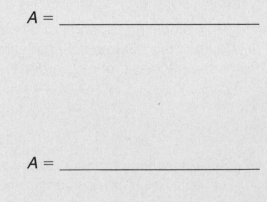

A = _____

4.

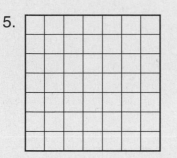

$A =$ _____

5.

$A =$ _____

6. Linda is laying tile in a hallway as shown in the figure below. Each tile is 1 square foot.

What is the area of the hallway that Linda is tiling? _____

7. Larry is building a patio. He is laying blocks that are 1 square foot as shown in the figure below.

What is the area of the patio Larry is building? _____

New York Math Practice

1 The size of Dawn's kitchen is shown below.

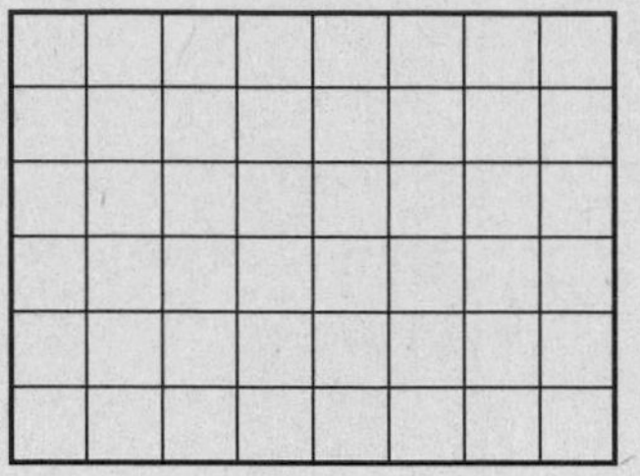

What is the area of Dawn's kitchen?

A 28 units

B 28 square units

C 48 units

D 48 square units

2 Chester's rectangular garden is 12 feet long and 8 feet wide. He wants to put bricks around its perimeter. He uses bricks that are 1 foot long. How many bricks will Chester need?

A 20

B 40

C 80

D 96

3   A playground has the shape of the figure below.

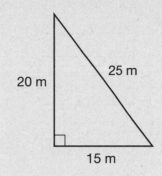

What is the perimeter of the playground?

A   40 meters

B   45 meters

C   60 meters

D   300 meters

4   What is the area of the shaded section?

A   12 square units

B   16 square units

C   28 square units

D   40 square units

5   Mark drew a square with a perimeter of 32 inches. What is the length of each side?

Show your work.

Answer: _____ inches

6 The garden Martina planted last year is shown below. Each square represents 1 square meter.

Part A

What was the perimeter of Martina's garden last year?

Answer: _____ meters

Part B

What was the area of Martina's garden last year?

Answer: _____ square meters

Part C

This year Martina makes her garden 2 meters longer and 2 meters wider. Make a drawing of Martina's garden.

Unit 4

Measurement

Have you ever been in a swimming pool and wondered how deep the water was, how long you were in the pool, or how much water the pool could hold? These are just a few examples of how measurement can be used in everyday life. You may not realize it, but every time you look at a clock for the time or stand on a scale to weigh yourself, you are measuring.

In this unit, you will learn about measuring length, mass, capacity, and time. You will convert measurements from one unit to another within the same measurement system. You will also learn about money.

In This Unit

Length

Mass and Capacity

Money and Time

Lesson 10: Length

When you want to know how long an object is, you measure its **length**. Length can be measured in **customary** or **metric units**. To measure length, you can use a **ruler**, a **yardstick** or **meterstick**, or a **tape measure**.

Customary Units

The most commonly used customary units of length are **inch, foot**, and **yard**.

1 inch (in.)
The diameter of a quarter
is about 1 inch.

about
1 in.

1 foot (ft) = 12 in.
The length of the longer side of a sheet
of notebook paper is about 1 foot.

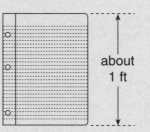
about
1 ft

1 yard (yd) = 3 ft
The height of a kitchen table
is about 1 yard.

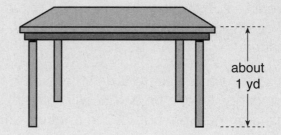
about
1 yd

Performance Indicators: 4.M.1, 4.M.3

Converting Customary Units of Length

You can find equivalent units of lengths by multiplying or dividing.

When finding an equivalent length with a smaller unit, multiply.

When finding an equivalent length with a larger unit, divide.

Example

How many feet are equivalent to 2 yards?
Feet are smaller units than yards, so multiply.

$$1 \text{ yd} = 3 \text{ ft}$$

$$2 \text{ yd} = 2 \times 3$$

$$2 \text{ yd} = 6 \text{ ft}$$

Example

How many feet are equivalent to 36 inches?
Feet are larger units than inches, so divide.

$$12 \text{ in.} = 1 \text{ ft}$$

$$36 \text{ in.} = ? \text{ ft}$$

$$36 \div 12 = 3$$

$$36 \text{ in.} = 3 \text{ ft}$$

Practice

Directions: For questions 1 through 5, write the customary unit that would be **best** to use to measure the length of each item.

1. an envelope _____

2. a field _____

3. a notebook _____

4. a screwdriver _____

5. an adult rattlesnake _____

Directions: For questions 6 through 13, make the correct conversions.

6. 12 ft = _____ yd

7. 72 in. = _____ ft

8. 36 ft = _____ in.

9. 48 in. = _____ ft

10. 96 ft = _____ yd

11. 7 ft = _____ in.

12. 24 yd = _____ ft

13. 24 in. = _____ ft

Directions: For questions 14 through 19, circle the **greater** length.

14. 3 yd   or   8 ft

15. 4 ft   or   60 in.

16. 16 ft   or   16 yd

17. 30 ft   or   6 yd

18. 2 ft   or   20 in.

19. 38 in.   or   4 ft

Measuring Length with an Inch Ruler

An inch ruler is used to measure items that are 1 foot or less. A ruler is divided into inches. Most rulers are further divided into fractions of an inch. The figure below shows $\frac{1}{4}$ and $\frac{1}{2}$ of an inch marked on an inch ruler.

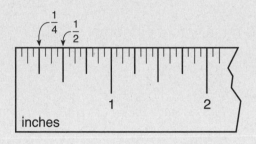

To the Nearest Inch

You can measure to the nearest inch by looking at which whole inch mark the end of the object is closest to.

Example

How long is this insect to the nearest inch?

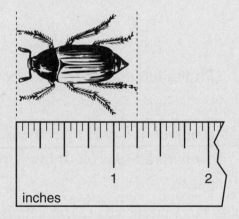

Step 1: **Line up the left edge of the ruler with the left edge of the object that you are measuring.**

Step 2: **Look at the inch mark that the right edge of the object is closest to.**

The right edge of the object is closest to the 1-inch mark. The insect is about 1 inch long.

To the Nearest Half-Inch

You can also measure to the nearest half-inch. You need to look at which $\frac{1}{2}$ mark the object is closest to. Sometimes it will be a $\frac{1}{2}$, and sometimes it will be a whole number.

Example

How long is this dragonfly to the nearest $\frac{1}{2}$ inch?

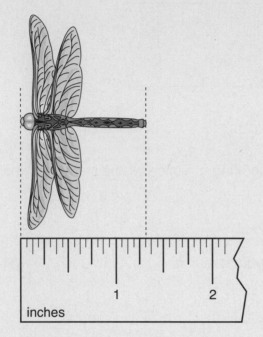

Step 1: **Line up the left edge of the ruler with the left edge of the object that you are measuring.**

Step 2: **Count the number of full inches the object has and then the number of $\frac{1}{2}$ inches past the last full inch. You will need to look at the $\frac{1}{2}$ mark that the right edge of the object is closest to.**

The line is closest to the $\frac{1}{2}$ mark after the 1 on the ruler. The length of the dragonfly is about $1\frac{1}{2}$ inches.

To the Nearest Quarter-Inch

You can also measure to the nearest quarter-inch. You need to look at which $\frac{1}{4}$ mark the object is closest to. It may be a $\frac{1}{4}$, $\frac{1}{2}$, $\frac{3}{4}$, or a whole number.

Example

How long is this insect to the nearest $\frac{1}{4}$ inch?

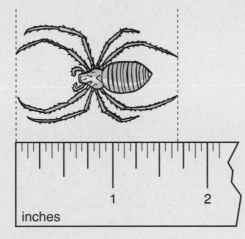

Step 1: **Line up the left edge of the ruler with the left edge of the object that you are measuring.**

Step 2: **Count the number of full inches the object has and then the number of $\frac{1}{4}$ inches past the last full inch. You will need to look at the $\frac{1}{4}$ mark that the right edge of the object is closest to.**

The line is closest to the third $\frac{1}{4}$ mark after the 1 on the ruler. The length of the insect is about $1\frac{3}{4}$ inches.

Practice

Directions: For questions 1 through 10, use an inch ruler to measure each object to the nearest unit given.

1. inch

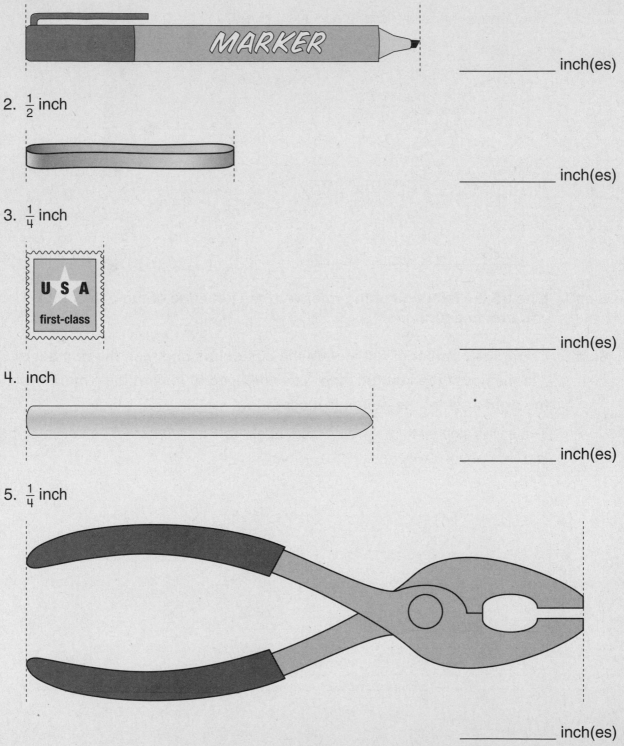

_____ inch(es)

2. $\frac{1}{2}$ inch

_____ inch(es)

3. $\frac{1}{4}$ inch

U S A
★
first-class

_____ inch(es)

4. inch

_____ inch(es)

5. $\frac{1}{4}$ inch

_____ inch(es)

Performance Indicator: 4.M.2

6. inch

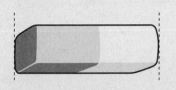

_____ inch(es)

7. $\frac{1}{2}$ inch

_____ inch(es)

8. $\frac{1}{4}$ inch

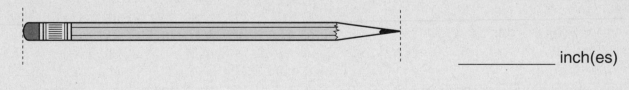

_____ inch(es)

9. $\frac{1}{2}$ inch

_____ inch(es)

10. $\frac{1}{2}$ inch

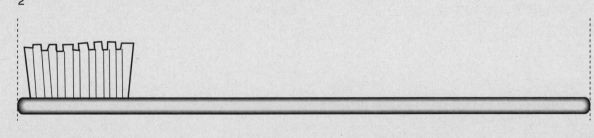

_____ inch(es)

Metric Units

The most commonly used metric units of length are **centimeter** and **meter**.

1 centimeter (cm)
The width of a large paper clip is
about 1 centimeter.

about
1 cm

1 meter (m) = 100 cm
The length of a Major League
baseball bat is about 1 meter.

about
1 m

Practice

Directions: For questions 1 through 3, write the metric unit that would be **better** to use to measure the length of each item.

1. a piece of chalk _____

2. a wall in your classroom _____

3. the floor in your bedroom _____

Directions: For questions 4 through 6, write an estimate for the length of each item using the unit given.

4. a wall in your classroom: _____ meters

5. the distance across your desk: _____ centimeters

6. a basketball court: _____ meters

Performance Indicator: 4.M.2

Measuring Length with a Centimeter Ruler

A metric ruler is used to measure items that are 1 meter or less in length. A meterstick is used to measure longer items. Each meter is divided into 100 centimeters.

Example

How long is this crayon to the nearest centimeter?

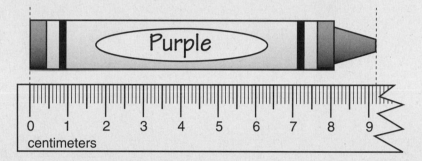

Step 1: **Line up the 0 centimeter mark on the ruler with the left edge of the object that you are measuring.**

Step 2: **Count the number of full centimeters.**

The end of the crayon is closest to the 9 on the ruler. The length of the crayon is about 9 centimeters.

TIP: Some rulers measure both inches and centimeters. These rulers have inches on one side and centimeters on the other side.

Practice

Directions: For questions 1 through 8, use a centimeter ruler to measure each object to the nearest centimeter.

1.

_____ centimeters

2.

_____ centimeters

165

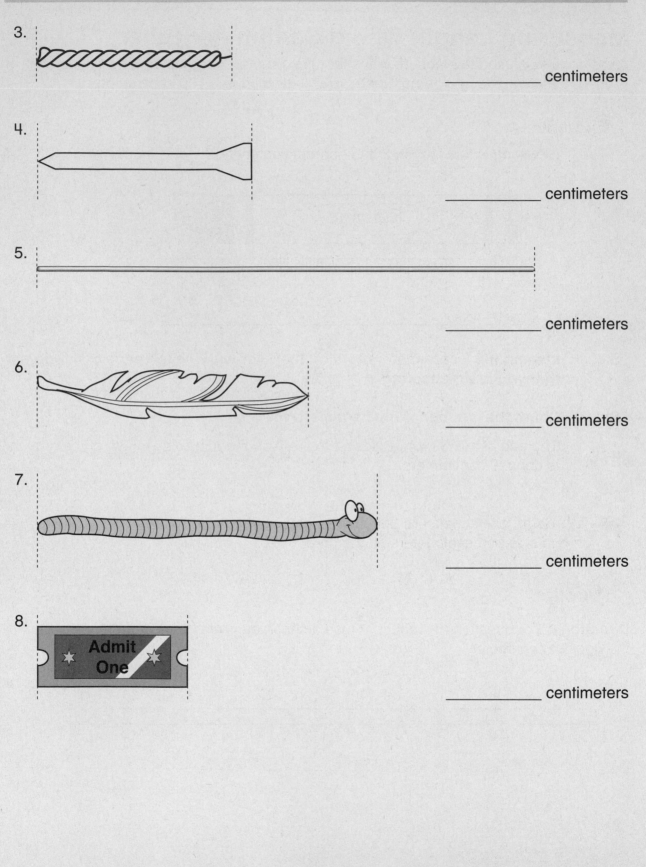

3. _____ centimeters

4. _____ centimeters

5. _____ centimeters

6. _____ centimeters

7. _____ centimeters

8. _____ centimeters

New York Math Practice

1 Which is the **best** estimate of the length of a cell phone?

   A 10 centimeters

   B 100 centimeters

   C 1 meter

   D 10 meters

2 Lucy planted a garden that is 24 feet long. How many **yards** long is Lucy's garden?

   A 2

   B 8

   C 72

   D 288

3 Use your ruler to help you solve this problem.

Which is the length of this nail to the nearest inch?

   A 3

   B $3\frac{1}{2}$

   C $3\frac{3}{4}$

   D 4

4 Matt and Kevin are measuring the length of their classroom. Which tool and customary unit would be best for them to use?

A   centimeter ruler; centimeters

B   inch ruler; inches

C   inch ruler; feet

D   yardstick; yards

5 Pam measures 4 dogs. Their heights are shown in the table.

Dog	Height
Rover	28 inches
Max	1 yard
Fido	18 inches
Tippy	2 feet

Which list shows the dogs in order from **shortest** to **tallest**?

A   Fido, Tippy, Rover, Max

B   Max, Rover, Tippy, Fido

C   Max, Tippy, Fido, Rover

D   Tippy, Fido, Max, Rover

6 Miranda is buying a tablecloth for her kitchen table. Which is the **best** estimate of the length of a kitchen table?

A 2 feet

B 6 feet

C 20 feet

D 60 feet

7 Use your ruler to help you solve this problem.

Ted uses this size battery in his toothbrush.

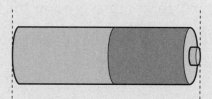

Which is the length of the battery to the nearest centimeter?

A 3

B 4

C 5

D 6

8 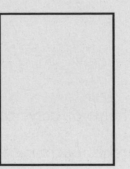 Use your ruler to help you solve this problem.

Carlos drew the rectangle shown below.

Which is the distance, in centimeters, around the rectangle?

A   7

B   10

C   12

D   14

9 Use your ruler to help you solve this problem.

Maya is making a puppet. She cut pieces of yarn this length to use for hair.

What is the length of the yarn to the nearest $\frac{1}{2}$ inch?

Answer: _____ inches

What is the length of the yarn to the nearest $\frac{1}{4}$ inch?

Answer: _____ inches

Performance Indicators: 4.M.4, 4.M.5

Lesson 11: Mass and Capacity

When you want to know how much matter ("stuff") is in an object, you measure its **mass**. Mass can be measured in metric units. To measure mass, you can use a **scale** or **balance**.

When you want to know how much liquid an object can hold, you measure its **capacity**. Capacity can be measured in metric units. To measure capacity, you can use measuring cups.

Mass

The most commonly used metric units of mass are **gram** and **kilogram**.

1 gram (g)
A paper clip has a mass of about 1 gram.

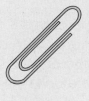

1 kilogram (kg) = 1,000 g
A pineapple has a mass of about 1 kilogram.

Example

A coconut is placed on one side of a balance scale. What is the mass of the coconut?

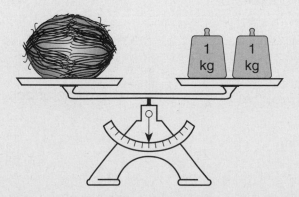

The scale balances when 2 kilogram masses are placed on the other side. So, the coconut has a mass of 2 kilograms.

Practice

Directions: For questions 1 and 2, write the mass of the given item. Be sure to label the units used.

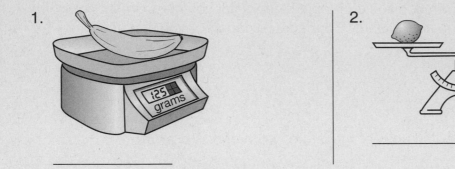

1. _____

2. _____

Directions: For questions 3 through 6, fill in the table with real-world objects. First, estimate the mass of the objects using metric units. Then, measure each mass using metric units. Write in the units you used for your measurement.

	Object	Estimate	Measurement
3.			
4.			
5.			
6.			

Directions: For questions 7 through 10, write the metric unit that would be **best** to use to measure the mass of each item.

7. a bowling ball _____

8. a horse _____

9. an eyelash _____

10. a piece of paper _____

Capacity

Some commonly used metric units of capacity are **milliliter** and **liter**.

1 milliliter (mL)
This eyedropper shows about 1 milliliter.

1 liter (L) = 1,000 mL
The capacity of this kind of carton is about 1 liter.

To measure capacity, you can use **measuring cups** or **beakers**.

Example

How much liquid is in the measuring cup?

```
600 — mL
500 — mL
400 — mL
300 — mL
200 — mL
100 — mL
```

The top of the liquid is halfway between the marks for 400 mL and 500 mL.
450 is halfway between 400 and 500, so there are 450 mL of liquid in the
measuring cup.

Practice

Directions: For questions 1 through 4, fill in the table with real-world objects. First, estimate the capacity of the objects using metric units. Then, measure their capacities using metric units. Write in the units you used for your measurement.

	Object	Estimate	Measurement
1.			
2.			
3.			
4.			

Directions: For questions 5 through 10, write the metric unit that would be **best** to use to measure the capacity of each item.

5. a drinking straw _____

6. a car's gas tank _____

7. a soup spoon _____

8. coffee pot _____

9. a teacup _____

10. a swimming pool _____

Directions: For questions 11 through 13, fill in the blank with the most reasonable metric unit of capacity.

11. The capacity of a soup bowl is about 200 _____.

12. The capacity of a car's gas tank is about 60 _____.

13. A can of soda is about 350 _____.

New York Math Practice

1 Which animal's mass is **best** measured in grams?

   A cat

   B dog

   C hamster

   D parrot

2 Dr. Sato is measuring the mass of a newborn baby. Which tool is Dr. Sato using?

   A a scale

   B a ruler

   C a tape measure

   D a measuring cup

3 Nathan poured water into the beaker shown below.

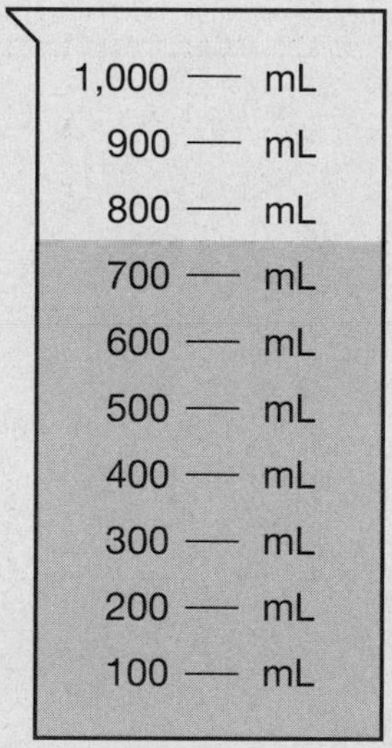

| 1,000 — mL |
| 900 — mL |
| 800 — mL |
| 700 — mL |
| 600 — mL |
| 500 — mL |
| 400 — mL |
| 300 — mL |
| 200 — mL |
| 100 — mL |

About how much water is in the beaker?

   A 700 mL

   B 710 mL

   C 750 mL

   D 800 mL

4   Which object's capacity is **best** measured using liters?

   A   drinking glass

   B   kitchen sink

   C   soup bowl

   D   coffee mug

5   Which metric unit would be **best** to use to measure the mass of a car?

   A   gram

   B   meter

   C   liter

   D   kilogram

6   Sarah is measuring the mass of some items in her classroom. What is the mass of the scissors shown below?

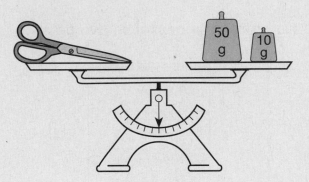

Show your work.

Answer: _____ grams

Lesson 12: Money and Time

U.S. money is written in dollars and cents. Use a dollar sign ($) or a cents sign (¢) to identify a money amount.

Counting Money

To count money, always start with the bill or coin of greatest value.

Example

What is the total value of the amount of money?

Start with the quarters. Add the amounts as you go from left to right.

25 + 25 + 10 + 10 + 10 + 5 + 5 + 1 + 1 = 92

The total value is ninety-two cents, 92¢, or $0.92.

Example

What is the total value of the amount of money?

Count the bills, starting from the greatest value. Then count the coins, starting from the greatest value. Then add the totals of the bills and coins together.

bills: 5 + 1 + 1 + 1 = $8

coins: 25 + 25 + 1 = 51¢ ($0.51)

total: $8 + $0.51 = $8.51

The total value is eight dollars and fifty-one cents, or $8.51.

Practice

Directions: For questions 1 through 7, write the value of the money shown.

1.

_____

2.

_____

3.

_____

4.

_____

5.

_____

6.

_____

7.

_____

Making Change

Change is the amount of money you get back when you make a payment that is more than the cost of an item. To make change, count up from the cost of the item to the dollar amount used to pay for the item. You can also subtract to make change.

Example

Sallie bought a box of mixed nuts for $3.59. She gave the clerk $10.00. How much change will Sallie get back?

Start with the cost of the box of mixed nuts. Then count the coins and bills until you reach the amount Sallie gave the clerk.

| $3.59 | $3.60 | $3.65 | $3.75 | $4.00 |

| $5.00 | $10.00 |

Sallie will get $6.41 back in change.

You can also use subtraction to find out how much change Sallie will get back.

Example

Write the cost of the box of mixed nuts under the amount Sallie gave the clerk. Line up the decimal points.

$$\begin{array}{r} \$10.00 \\ -\ \ \$3.59 \\ \end{array}$$

Subtract. Borrow and regroup when necessary.

$$\begin{array}{r} \overset{9\ \ 9\,10}{\$\cancel{10}.\cancel{00}} \\ -\ \ \$3.59 \\ \hline \$6.41 \end{array}$$

Sallie will get $6.41 back in change.

ractice

1. Patti bought a carnation for $0.84. She gave the clerk the amount of money shown below. How much change did Patti get back?

_____

2. Chris bought a comic book for $3.46. He gave the clerk $5. How much change did Chris get back?

_____

3. Jade bought a skirt for $17.47. She gave the clerk $20. How much change did Jade get back?

_____

4. Brent bought a pen for $1.24. He gave the clerk $2. How much change did Brent get back?

_____

5. Stephen bought a used CD for $4.76. He gave the clerk $10.01. How much change did Stephen get back?

_____

6. Kristi bought an MP3 player that cost $56.45. She paid with bills that totaled $60.00. How much change should Kristi get back?

_____

7. While on vacation, the Koya family bought 4 T-shirts that cost $12 each. They also bought a set of postcards for $5. They gave the store clerk $60.00. How much money should the Koya family get back in change?

_____

Elapsed Time

The time that passes from the start of an activity to the end of it is called **elapsed time**. To find elapsed time, you need to understand hours and minutes.

◢ Example

How much time elapsed from 2:30 to 5:00?

Starting Time   Ending Time

Count how many times the long hand makes one trip all the way around the clock.

2:30 to 3:30 = one trip = 1 hour

3:30 to 4:30 = another trip = 1 hour

The long hand made **2** trips around the clock. This is **2** hours.

Now find the remaining part of an hour.

Count by five starting at 4:30 and stopping at 5:00.

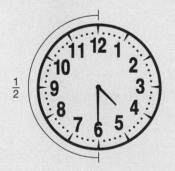

There are 30 minutes between 4:30 and 5:00. The long hand made $\frac{1}{2}$ trip around the clock. This is $\frac{1}{2}$ hour.

2 hours 30 minutes or $2\frac{1}{2}$ hours elapsed from 2:30 to 5:00.

Performance Indicator: 4.M.9

Practice

1. Sheila arrived at school at the time shown on the digital clock on the left. She ate lunch at the time shown on the digital clock on the right.

Arrived   Lunch

How long was Sheila at school until she ate lunch? _____

2. Ben left his house at 12:30 P.M. and arrived at his grandmother's house in Schenectady at 2:00 P.M.

Left   Arrived

How long did Ben's trip take? _____

3. Matt's basketball game starts at the time shown on this analog clock.

Matt's coach wants the team to arrive at the gym $\frac{1}{2}$ hour before the game starts. It takes Matt $\frac{1}{2}$ hour to ride his bike from his house to the gym. What is the latest time that Matt can leave home and still arrive at the gym when his coach wants him to?

_____

4. Monica arrived at ballet lessons at the time shown on the digital clock on the left. She left ballet lessons at the time shown on the digital clock on the right.

Arrived   Left

How long was Monica at ballet lessons? _____

5. John left his house at 9:00 A.M. and arrived at the airport at 11:30 A.M.

Left   Arrived

How long did it take John to get to the airport?

_____

6. James left his house at 7:30 A.M. and arrived at the grocery store at 8:00 A.M. How long did it take James to get to the grocery store?

A. $\frac{1}{2}$ hour

B. 1 hour

C. $1\frac{1}{2}$ hours

D. $15\frac{1}{2}$ hours

7. Andrea started jogging at 5:00 A.M. and finished at 6:30 A.M. How long was Andrea jogging?

A. $\frac{1}{2}$ hour

B. 1 hour

C. $1\frac{1}{2}$ hours

D. $11\frac{1}{2}$ hours

Calendars

Time is also measured in **days, weeks, months,** and **years.** You can use a **calendar** to keep track of these longer units of time.

November						
Sun.	Mon.	Tues.	Wed.	Thurs.	Fri.	Sat.
	1	2	3	4	5	6
7	8	9	10	11	12	13
14	15	16	17	18	19	20
21	22	23	24	25	26	27
28	29	30				

December						
Sun.	Mon.	Tues.	Wed.	Thurs.	Fri.	Sat.
			1	2	3	4
5	6	7	8	9	10	11
12	13	14	15	16	17	18
19	20	21	22	23	24	25
26	27	28	29	30	31	

1 day = 24 hours

7 days = 1 week

28–31 days = 1 month

12 months = 1 year

Example

On November 16, Abbey has her first basketball game. On December 7, she has her second basketball game. How many days after the first basketball game is the second one?

Look at the calendar and find November 16. You can count the number of days until December 7.

The second basketball game is 21 days after the first basketball game.

You can also count the number of weeks. December 7 is exactly 3 weeks after November 16. You know that there are 7 days in 1 week.

$3 \times 7 = 21$

The second basketball game is 3 weeks, or 21 days, after the first one.

Practice

Directions: Use the calendars to answer questions 1 through 5.

February						
Sun.	Mon.	Tues.	Wed.	Thurs.	Fri.	Sat.
					1	2
3	4	5	6	7	8	9
10	11	12	13	14	15	16
17	18	19	20	21	22	23
24	25	26	27	28	29	

March						
Sun.	Mon.	Tues.	Wed.	Thurs.	Fri.	Sat.
						1
2	3	4	5	6	7	8
9	10	11	12	13	14	15
16	17	18	19	20	21	22
23	24	25	26	27	28	29
30	31					

1. How many days are there from February 5 to March 19? _____

2. How many weeks and days are there from February 22 to March 8? _____

3. On February 18, John received an invitation to a party. The date of the party is March 12. How many days before the party did John receive the invitation?

   _____

4. Callie has basketball practice every Tuesday in February. How many times does she have basketball practice in February?

   _____

5. Mike's family eats chicken noodle soup for dinner every 16 days. If they eat chicken noodle soup for dinner on February 21, on what day of the week will they eat chicken noodle soup the next time?

   _____

   What is the date of that day? _____

New York Math Practice

1 Isabelle bought a deck of playing cards for $2.18. She gave the clerk 3 one-dollar bills. Which set of coins would be Isabelle's correct change?

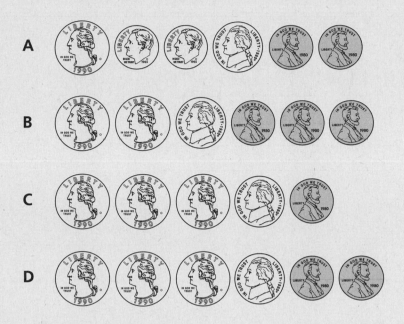

2 Jamal plays the violin. He practiced from the time shown on the clock on the left to the time shown on the clock on the right. For how long did Jamal practice the violin?

Start   Finish

A $\frac{1}{2}$ hour

B 1 hour

C $1\frac{1}{2}$ hours

D 6 hours

3   It is August 5. How many weeks is it until August 26?

August

Sun.	Mon.	Tues.	Wed.	Thurs.	Fri.	Sat.
					1	2
3	4	5	6	7	8	9
10	11	12	13	14	15	16
17	18	19	20	21	22	23
24/31	25	26	27	28	29	30

A 2

B 3

C 14

D 21

4   Marla bought a basketball for $18.45. She paid for it with $20.00. Which set of bills and coins could be Marla's correct change?

5 A special exhibit opens at a museum on March 6. It stays open for 6 weeks and 2 days. On what date does the exhibit close?

March						
Sun.	Mon.	Tues.	Wed.	Thurs.	Fri.	Sat.
1	2	3	4	5	6	7
8	9	10	11	12	13	14
15	16	17	18	19	20	21
22	23	24	25	26	27	28
29	30	31				

April						
Sun.	Mon.	Tues.	Wed.	Thurs.	Fri.	Sat.
			1	2	3	4
5	6	7	8	9	10	11
12	13	14	15	16	17	18
19	20	21	22	23	24	25
26	27	28	29	30		

A April 12

B April 17

C April 19

D April 26

6 Mr. Williams bought a ticket to a concert for $42.50. He paid for the ticket with $50.00. How much change did he get back?

Show your work.

Answer: _____

7   Lulu arrived at the gym at 3:00 P.M. She left the gym at 4:30 P.M.

Part A

How long was Lulu at the gym?

$$\begin{array}{r} 4:30 \\ -\ 3:00 \\ \hline 1:30 \end{array}$$

Answer: _____1hr 30min_____

Part B

Lulu took a yoga class that lasted for 30 minutes. How much time did she have left to spend in the exercise room?

$$\begin{array}{r} 1:30 \\ -\ \ 30 \\ \hline 1:00 \end{array}$$

Answer: _____1hr_____

Part C

It took $\frac{1}{2}$ hour for Lulu to get home after she left the gym. What time did Lulu get home?

30mi

$$\begin{array}{r} 4:30 \\ +\ 30 \\ \hline 5:00 \end{array}$$

Answer: _____5:00 pm_____

Unit 5

Statistics and Probability

By organizing data, you can find out things such as how many of your classmates like to go hiking, who read the most books over summer vacation, or what kinds of vegetables your classmates like to eat. Probability is a way of predicting and showing all the possible ways something can turn out.

In this unit, you will learn how to collect, organize, display, and understand data by answering questions about tables and graphs. You will also make conclusions and predictions from data and graphs.

In this Unit
Data Collection and
Analysis

Lesson 13: Data Collection and Analysis

Data is information. It can be collected, organized, and analyzed.

Collecting Data

Data can be collected by observation or survey.

- In an **observation,** you watch an event taking place in the world and record what you see.

- In a **survey,** you ask a group of people one or more questions. The questions should lead to specific answers.

Example

Suzi observed her classmates to see how many of them write left-handed (LH) or right-handed (RH). Her results are shown below.

RH, LH, RH, LH, LH, RH, RH, LH, RH, RH, RH, RH, RH, LH

Suzi found that 9 of her classmates write right-handed, and 5 of her classmates write left-handed.

Example

Tamika asked each member of her family to name his or her favorite color. Her results are shown below.

blue, red, orange, blue, blue, red, blue, green, purple

Tamika found that, in her family, 4 people like blue, 2 people like red, 1 person likes orange, 1 person likes green, and 1 person likes purple.

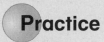 **Practice**

1. Write down the number of siblings of each of your classmates.

   _____

   _____

   _____

   How many siblings do the greatest number of your classmates have?

   _____

2. Ask your classmates the following survey question: "What is your favorite season of the year?" (The seasons are winter, spring, summer, and fall.) Write down the seasons that your classmates give.

   _____

   _____

   _____

   Which season is the favorite of most of your classmates?

   _____

   Which season is the favorite of the fewest of your classmates?

   _____

3. Look at your classmates. Write down the hair color of each of your classmates.

   _____

   _____

   _____

   What hair color do the greatest number of your classmates have?

   _____

   What hair color do the least number of your classmates have?

   _____

Tables

When you collect data, it is useful to organize it so that it is easier for others to read. One way to organize data is in a table.

▲ Example

Tina asked each student in her class this question: *"What kinds of pets do you own?"* Here are her results:

cat, fish, dog, dog, bird, no pet, dog, cat, cat, hamster, no pet, cat, dog, fish, hamster, fish, dog, cat, dog, fish

Tina counted how many times each answer was given. Then she organized her data into the table below.

**Kinds of Pets
Owned by Students
in Tina's Class**

Pet	Number of Students
Bird	1
Cat	5
Dog	6
Fish	4
Hamster	2
No pet	2

One of Tina's classmates said that he is getting a new pet. Based on the data Tina collected, what kind of pet is he most likely to get?

The table shows that 6 students have a dog. This is the greatest number of students shown in the table.

So, Tina's classmate is most likely to get a dog.

Practice

Directions: Use the information in the table below to answer questions 1 through 4.

Derek surveyed his fourth grade classmates about their favorite sport. The results are shown in the table below.

Favorite Sports of Students in Derek's Class

Sport	Number of Students
Baseball	5
Basketball	4
Hockey	3
Soccer	7
Swimming	2

1. How many students like basketball best?

   _____

2. Which is the least popular sport?

   _____

3. How many more students prefer baseball than prefer hockey?

   _____

4. Another fourth grader in Derek's school is asked to name his or her favorite sport. Which sport is he or she most likely to name?

   _____

Directions: Use the information in the table below to answer questions 5 through 7.

The table shows how 10 students scored on their last math test.

Math Test Scores

Student	Points
Grace	94
Abby	87
Parker	62
Sam	98
Payton	75
Ryan	68
Caleb	90
Hannah	79
Trey	84
Brynn	87

5. How many students scored 90 points or more?

   _____

6. How many students scored between 79 and 90?

   _____

7. Paula was absent on the day the test was given. She will take the test when she returns. Is she more likely to score above or below 80 points?

   _____

8. Renee asked each of the students in her class what his or her favorite type of movie is. Here are the results of her survey:

drama, comedy, drama, horror, drama, comedy, drama, animation, animation, comedy, horror, comedy, animation, comedy, comedy, drama, animation, comedy, horror, comedy, horror, drama

Fill in the following table with Renee's data.

Favorite Movie Types

Movie Types	Number of Students
Animation	
Comedy	
Drama	
Horror	

Directions: Use the table you completed in question 8 to answer questions 9 through 13.

9. How many students like a drama the best? _____

10. How many students answered the survey? _____

11. How many more students prefer comedy than prefer drama? _____

12. Which two types of movie do the same number of students like best?

_____

13. One student in Renee's class is going to a theater complex that is showing one of each type of movie listed in the table. Which type of movie will the student most likely attend? Explain your answer.

_____

_____

Bar Graphs

A **bar graph** uses bars to show data. Bar graphs are used to compare amounts of similar things.

Example

The bar graph below shows the number of students who participate in each of four after-school activities.

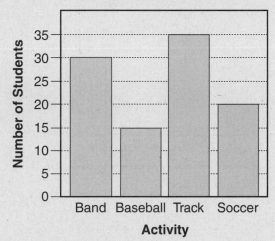

After-School Activities

In which after-school activity do 15 students participate?

Find 15 on the scale along the left side of the graph. Follow the horizontal line from 15 across the graph. The bar for *Baseball* ends at the line for 15.

The after-school activity that 15 students participate in is baseball.

How many more students participate in soccer than in baseball?

The bar for *Soccer* ends at 20. The bar for *Baseball* ends at 15.

$20 - 15 = 5$

Five more students participate in soccer than in baseball.

Practice

Directions: Use the following information to answer questions 1 through 5.

The graph below shows the number of fourth graders at one school who visited these four New York vacation spots.

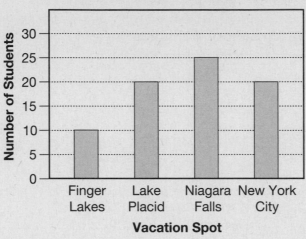

New York State Vacation Spots

1. How many students visited Lake Placid? _____

2. Which vacation spot did 10 students visit? _____

3. If each student visited only one vacation spot, how many students visited a vacation spot shown in the graph?

   _____

4. Which two vacation spots were visited by the same number of students?

   _____

5. Melinda is a fourth grader. This summer she will visit one of the vacation spots shown in the graph. Which spot is she most likely to visit? Explain your answer.

   _____

   _____

Directions: Use the following information to answer questions 6 through 8.

Ron kept track of the color of shirt of each student in his class. He recorded the results in the table below.

Color of Shirt

Color	Number of Students
Blue	8
Black	5
Red	4
Pink	7
White	6

6. Make a bar graph of the data.

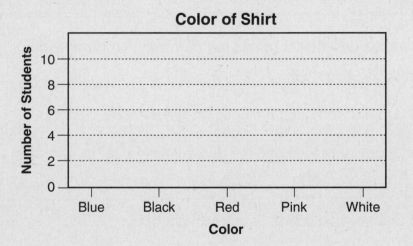

Color of Shirt

7. What color occurs most often? _____

8. If one more student enters Ron's class, what color do you think his or her shirt will be? Explain your answer.

_____

_____

Pictographs

A **pictograph** uses pictures or symbols to show data. The key will show you what each picture represents. The title of a pictograph is chosen by identifying the topic of the data.

Example

Maya and her dad went bass fishing. The pictograph shows how many bass they caught each day.

Bass Caught

Wednesday	🐟 🐟 🐟
Thursday	🐟 🐟 🐟 🐟
Friday	🐟 🐟 🐟 🐟 🐟 🐟
Saturday	🐟 🐟

KEY
🐟 = 2 fish

How many bass did Maya and her dad catch on Wednesday?

🐟 + 🐟 + 🐟 = 2 + 2 + 2 = 6

Maya and her dad caught 6 bass on Wednesday.

On what day did Maya and her dad catch 4 bass?

4 = 2 + 2 = 🐟 + 🐟

Maya and her dad caught 4 bass on Saturday.

Practice

Directions: Use the pictograph above to answer questions 1 through 3.

1. On what day did Maya and her dad catch the most bass? _____

2. How many more bass did Maya and her dad catch on Friday than on Wednesday?

   _____

3. How many bass did Maya and her dad catch in all? _____

Directions: Use the following information to answer questions 4 through 8.

The pictograph below shows the points Brittany scored in four basketball games.

Points Brittany Scored in Basketball Games

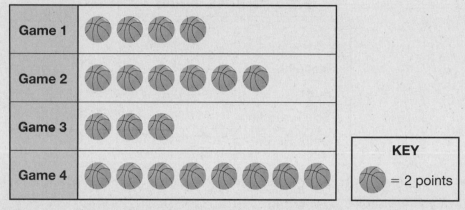

4. In which game did Brittany score the fewest points? _____

5. In which game did Brittany score 8 points? _____

6. In which game did Brittany score twice as many points as in Game 3?

_____

7. How many more points did Brittany score in Game 4 than in Game 2?

_____

8. How many points did Brittany score altogether in these four games?

_____

Directions: Use the following information to answer questions 9 through 11.

Ben asked all of the fourth graders in his school to name their favorite type of book. The results of his survey are shown in the table below.

Favorite Book Types

Book Type	Number of Students
Biography	15
Poetry	10
Science Fiction	25
Other Fiction	20

9. Complete the pictograph of the data. Give the pictograph a title. Make a key to show what each picture represents.

Book Type	Number of Students
Biography	
Poetry	
Science Fiction	
Other Fiction	

KEY

10. Explain why you chose the picture and the key that you used.

_____

_____

11. A new fourth grader comes to Ben's school. What type of book is most likely his or her least favorite? Explain your answer.

_____

_____

Line Graphs

A **line graph** can be used to show how data change over a period of time.

▲ Example

The line graph shows the amount in sales the Comic Connection made over a 10-week period.

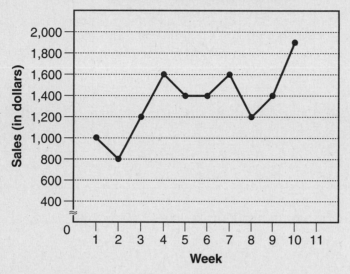

Comic Connection Sales

Between which two weeks in a row was there no change in weekly sales?

The segment of a line graph that slants up or down shows an increase or decrease.

The segment of a line graph that is flat and does not go up or down shows no change.

The segment from week 5 to week 6 is flat.

There was no change in weekly sales between weeks 5 and 6.

Between which two weeks in a row was there the greatest increase in sales? How much was the increase?

The segment from week 9 to week 10 is the steepest segment that shows an increase.

Sales for week 9 were $1,400. Sales for week 10 were $1,900.

Subtract to find the difference: $1,900 - 1,400 = 500$

The greatest increase in sales occurred between weeks 9 and 10. Sales increased by $500.

Practice

Directions: Use the line graph below to answer questions 1 through 4.

The line graph shows the profit Mrs. Smith made over a 6-day period selling vegetables.

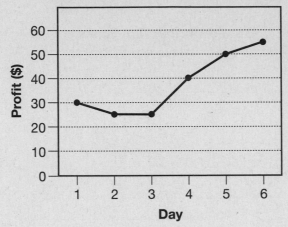

Mrs. Smith's Vegetable Sales

1. What is the amount of increase in profit from day 1 to day 6? _____

2. Between which two days in a row was there no change in profit?

    _____

3. Between which two days in a row was there the greatest increase in profit?

    _____

4. Do you think the profit for day 7 will be higher or lower than for day 6? Explain your answer.

    _____

    _____

Directions: Use the line graph below to answer questions 5 through 8.

The line graph below shows the population of a small town over a 10-year period.

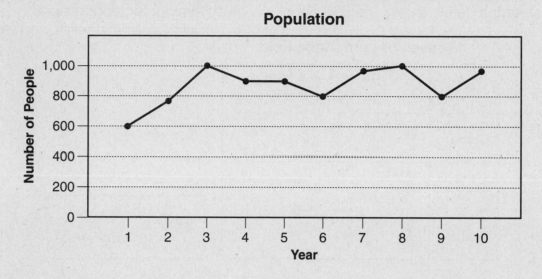

Population

5. Between which two years in a row was there no change in population?

_____

6. Between which two years in a row was there the greatest increase in population?

_____

7. By how much did the population increase from Year 1 to Year 8?

_____

8. Between which two years in a row was there the greatest decrease in population?

_____

New York Math Practice

Directions: Use the following information to answer questions 1 and 2.

The pictograph below shows the sales from the Miller family's lemonade stand.

Glasses of Lemonade Sold

Bo	🥤🥤🥤🥤🥤🥤
Carrie	🥤🥤🥤🥤
Scott	🥤
Vanessa	🥤🥤🥤

KEY
🥤 = 10 glasses sold

1 How many more glasses of lemonade did Bo sell than Carrie?

A 2

B 4

C 20

D 100

2 Scott decided to redraw the graph using the key shown below.

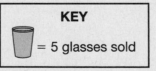

KEY
🥤 = 5 glasses sold

How many pictures should he draw to show the number of glasses of lemonade he sold?

A 1

B 2

C 5

D 10

Directions: Use the following information to answer questions 3 and 4.

Rajesh counted the different colors of vehicles that passed his house in one hour. His observations are shown in the table below.

Colors of Vehicles

Color	Number of Vehicles
Green	2
Silver	3
Black	7
Red	2
Gold	5
White	3

3 How many vehicles did Rajesh observe pass his house in one hour?

A 6

B 7

C 12

D 22

4 What color vehicle is **most** likely to drive by next?

A green

B silver

C black

D gold

5   The bar graph shows the number of minutes Lynne practiced the piano each day last week.

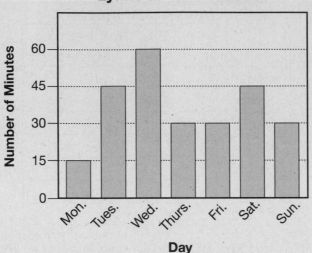

Lynne's Piano Practice

On what day did Lynne practice the **least** number of minutes?

A   Monday

B   Tuesday

C   Thursday

D   Friday

6   Juan wants to find out what his classmates like to do during the summer. Which question would be **best** for him to ask to find out?

A   Do you like swimming or bicycle riding better?

B   What is your favorite activity during the summer?

C   How often do you go to the beach?

D   Have you ever been to a water park?

Directions: Use the following information to answer questions 7 and 8.

Mr. Keller's math class is trying to collect 10,000 pop tabs. His class made the graph shown below to display how many tabs were collected in the first five weeks of this project.

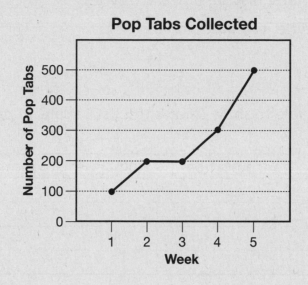

Pop Tabs Collected

7 Between which two weeks in a row was there the greatest increase in the number of pop tabs collected?

A weeks 1 and 2

B weeks 2 and 3

C weeks 3 and 4

D weeks 4 and 5

8 Do you think the number of pop tabs collected in week 6 will be greater or less than the number collected in week 5? Explain your answer.

Answer:

_____

_____

9 Sarah surveyed her classmates about the type of transportation they use to get to school. Here are her results:

bicycle, walking, bus, bus, car, car, bus,

walking, car, bus, bicycle, bus, car, bicycle,

bus, bus, bicycle, car, bus, car, bus

Part A

Complete the table to show Sarah's results. Be sure to give a title to the table.

Transportation	Number of Students

Part B

Make a bar graph to show Sarah's results.

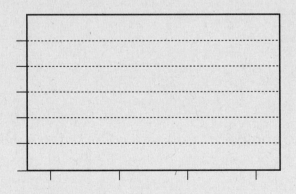

Part C

If one more student enters Sarah's class, what type of transportation do you think he or she **most** likely uses to get to school. Explain your answer.

Answer:

_____

_____

Notes

Notes

Notes

Notes

Notes

Notes

Notes

Notes